NORTH & SOUTH
IRELAND

BEFORE GOOD FRIDAY & THE CELTIC TIGER

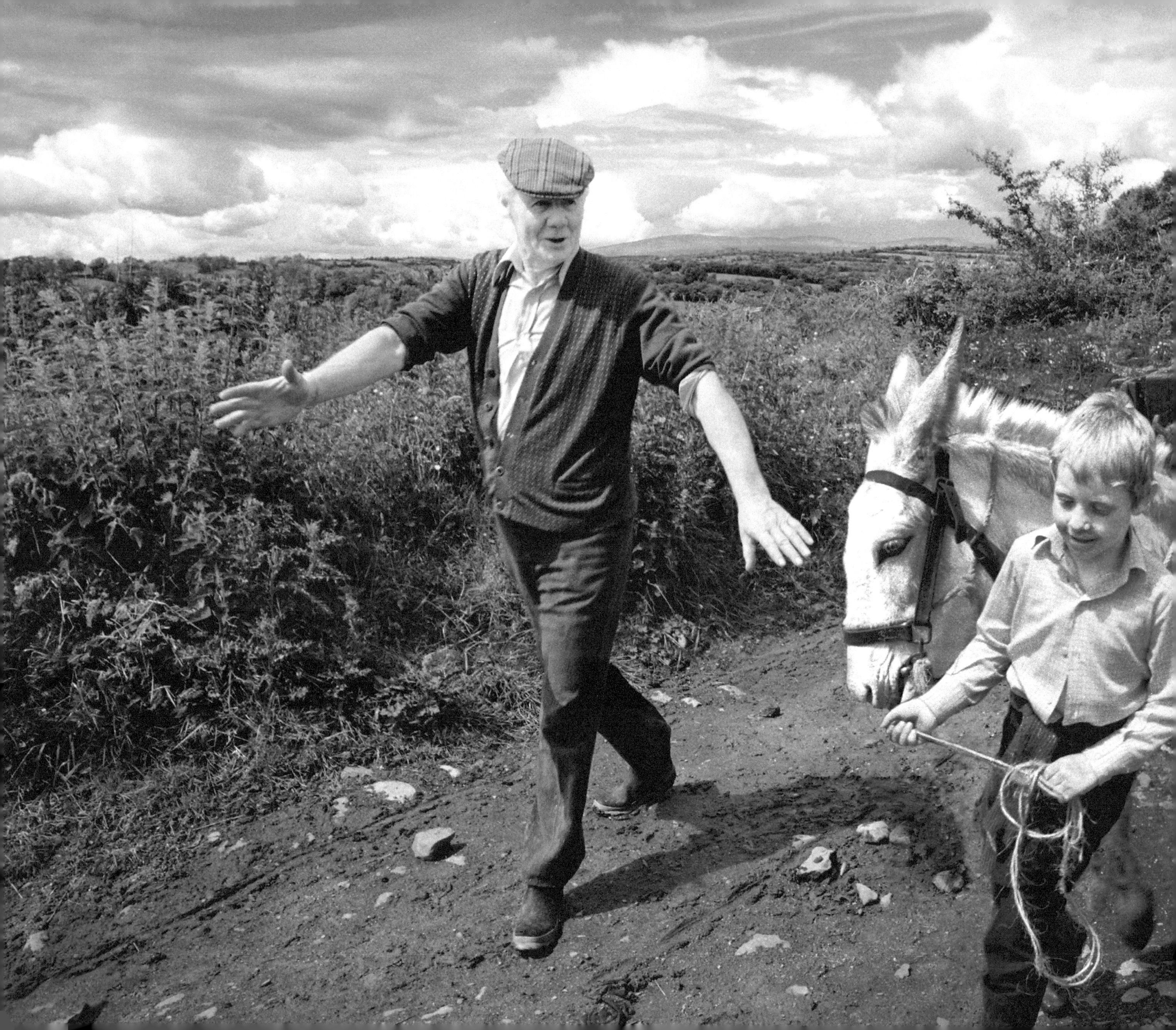

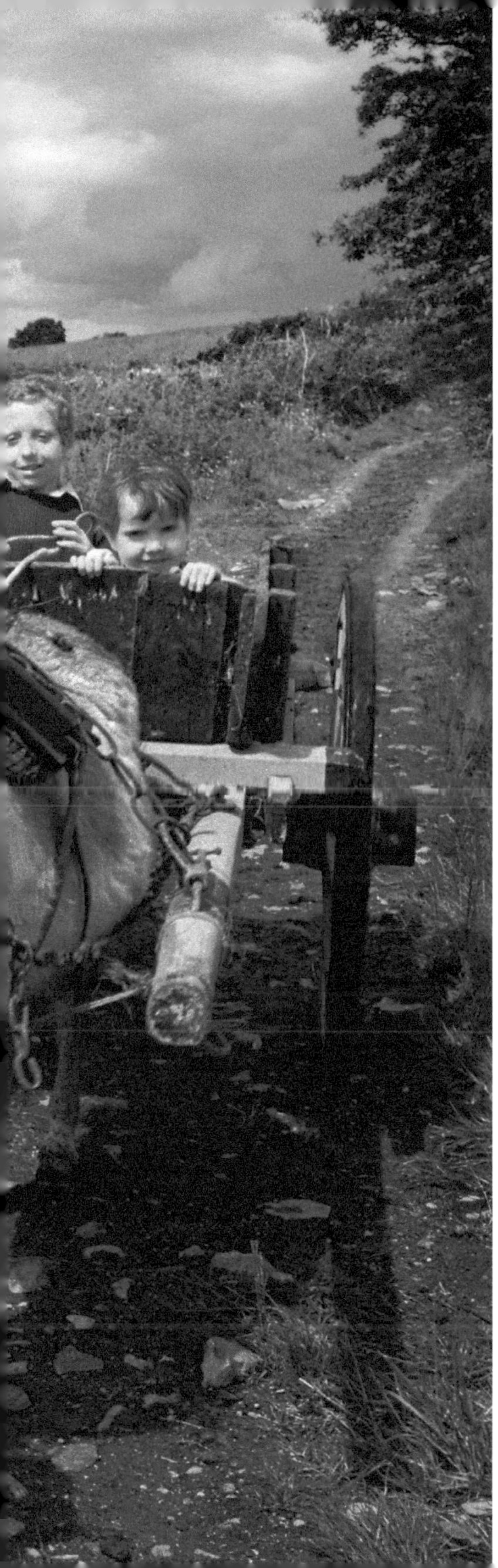

NORTH & SOUTH IRELAND

BEFORE GOOD FRIDAY & THE CELTIC TIGER

BY JAMES HIGGINS

INTRODUCTION BY STEPHEN O'CONNOR

Loom Press
Lowell, Massachusetts
2020

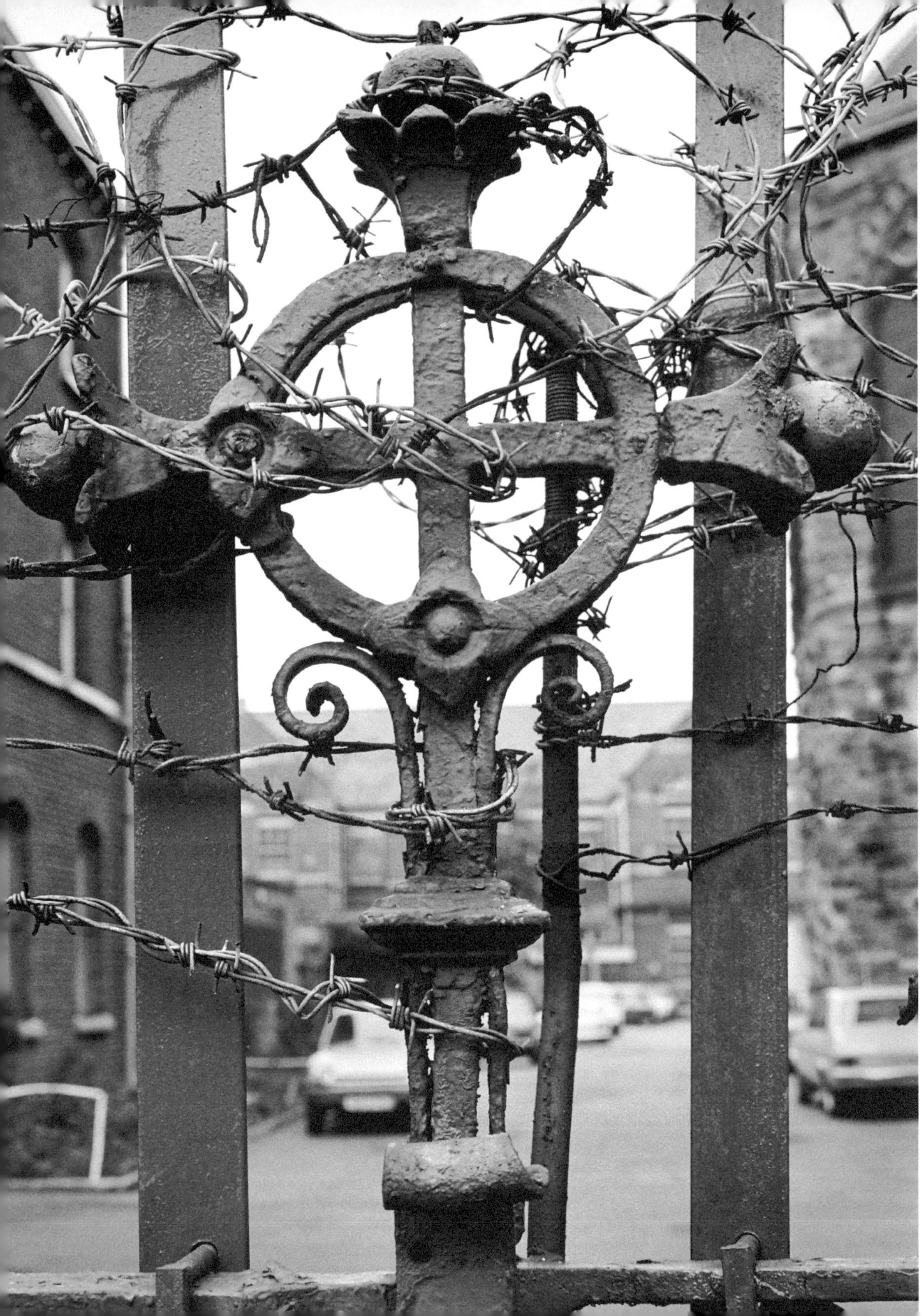

Church gate, Belfast, County Antrim,
Northern Ireland, 1982

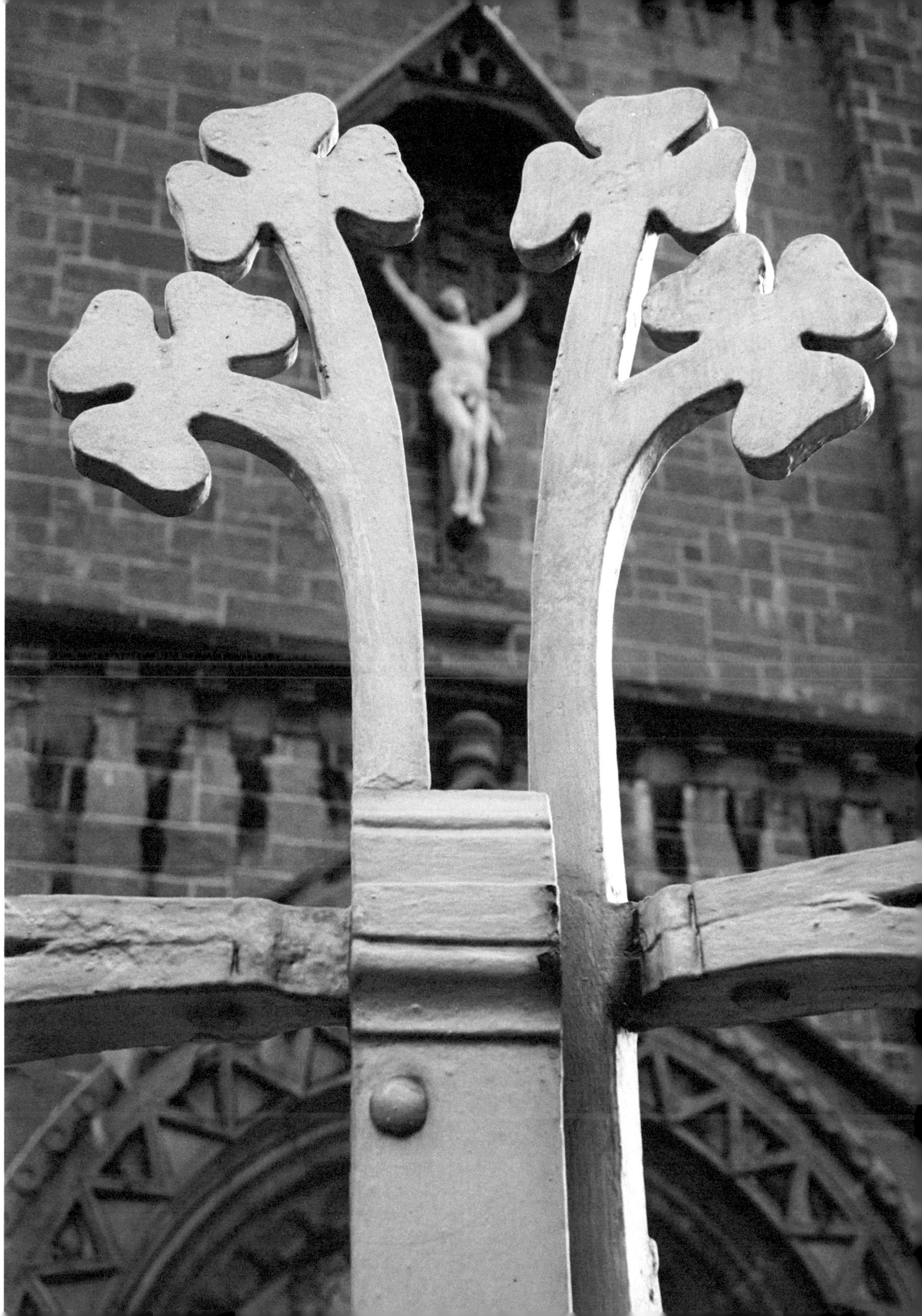

Church gate, Sligo City,
County Sligo, Ireland, 1982

Copyright © 2020 by James Higgins

ISBN 978-0-931507-51-9

All rights reserved. No part of this publication may be reproduced by any means existing or to be developed in the future without the written permission of the publisher except in the case of brief quotations embodied in critical articles and reviews.

Published in the United States of America
First edition

Loom Press
P.O. Box 1394
Lowell, MA 01853
info@loompress.com
www.loompress.com

Design: Joan Ross
Printing: King Printing Co., Inc. Lowell, Mass.

Cover image: Former school house, North of Portmagee, County Kerry, Ireland, 1983

Travel routes over a four-year period beginning in 1982, by plane, boat, car, and bicycle.

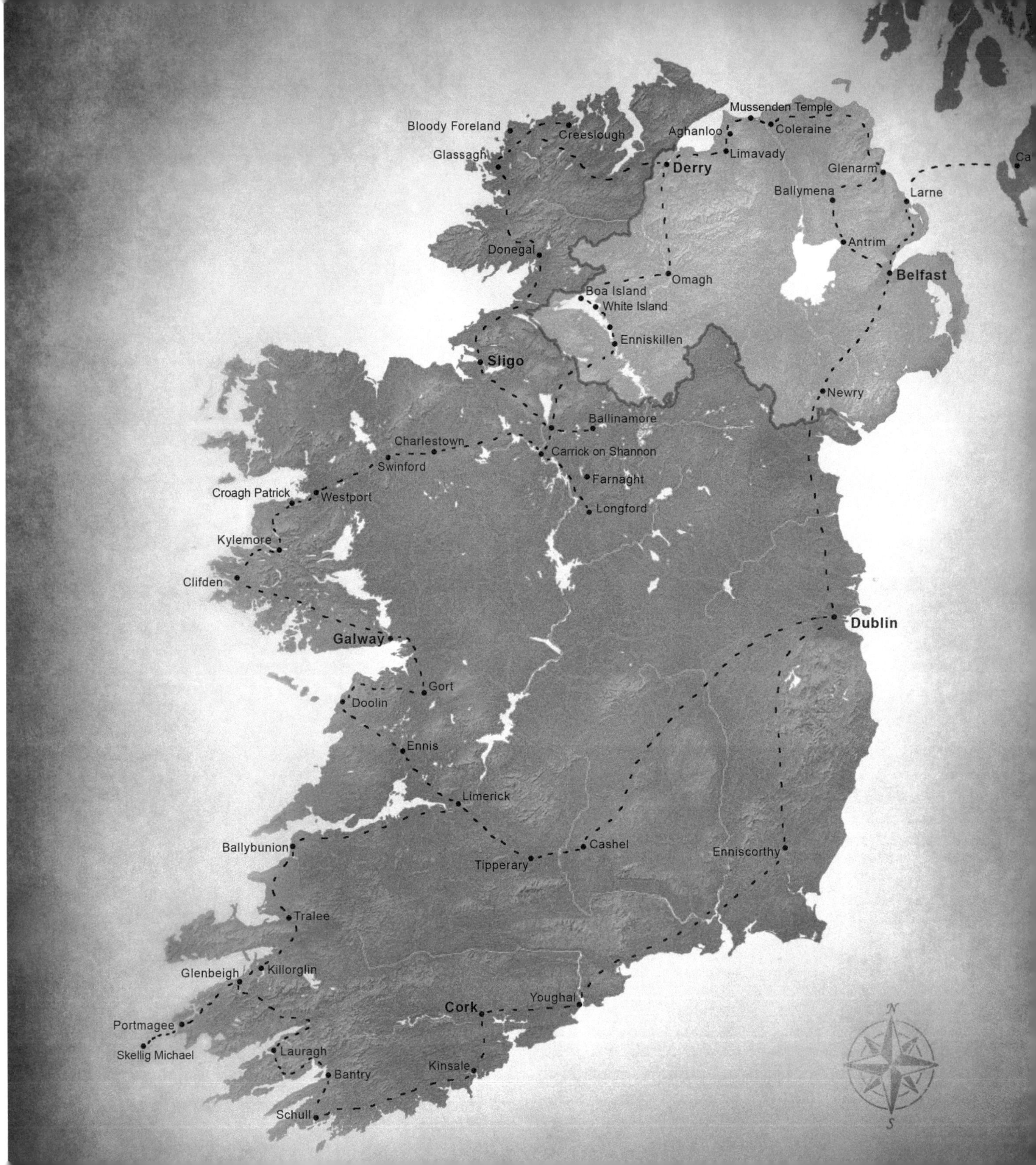

FOREWORD *by James Higgins*

I had no interest in visiting Ireland in 1982 when I flew to Scotland planning to photograph the Isle of Skye. Instead, when I got to Scotland, I headed south to Northern Ireland. Maybe it was the subliminal influence of Jill and Leon Uris' book, *Ireland a Terrible Beauty*.

The diversion was certainly not influenced by my family or so I thought at the time. My father came from a long line of Irish "cursed by the drink." His parents were born in Ireland and emigrated to the United States, and the curse came with them. My mother was an English-born tee-totaler who would come to regret marrying an Irishman. She disliked St. Patrick's Day and the Kennedys!

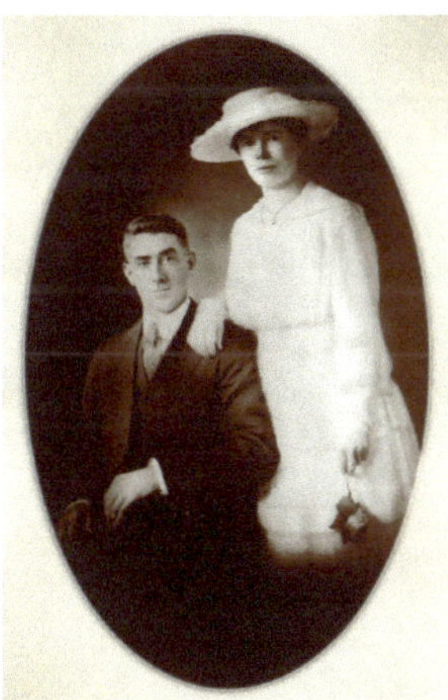

But for all the heartaches, brawling, and blarney, it was my Irish grandparents who gave me the gifts of curiosity and imagination—the possibilities of the "what ifs." And I'll always be grateful for that . . . .

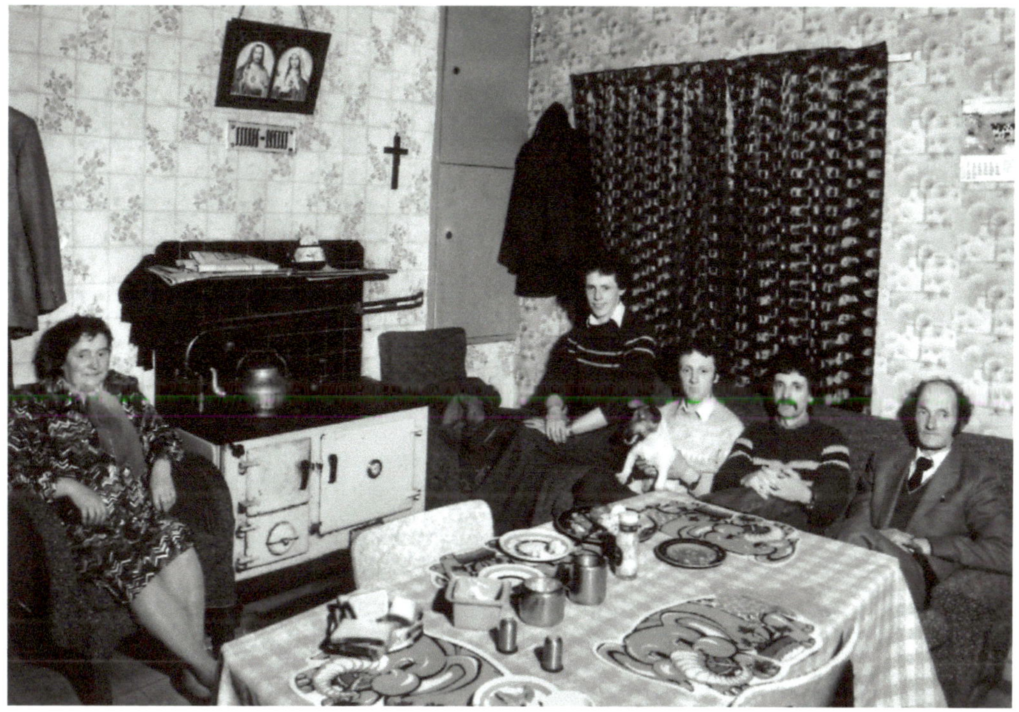

The author, second from right, with relatives Mary Doyle and family, Creenagh, County Leitrim, Ireland, 1983

Sinn Fein posters, Derry City, Northern Ireland, 1983

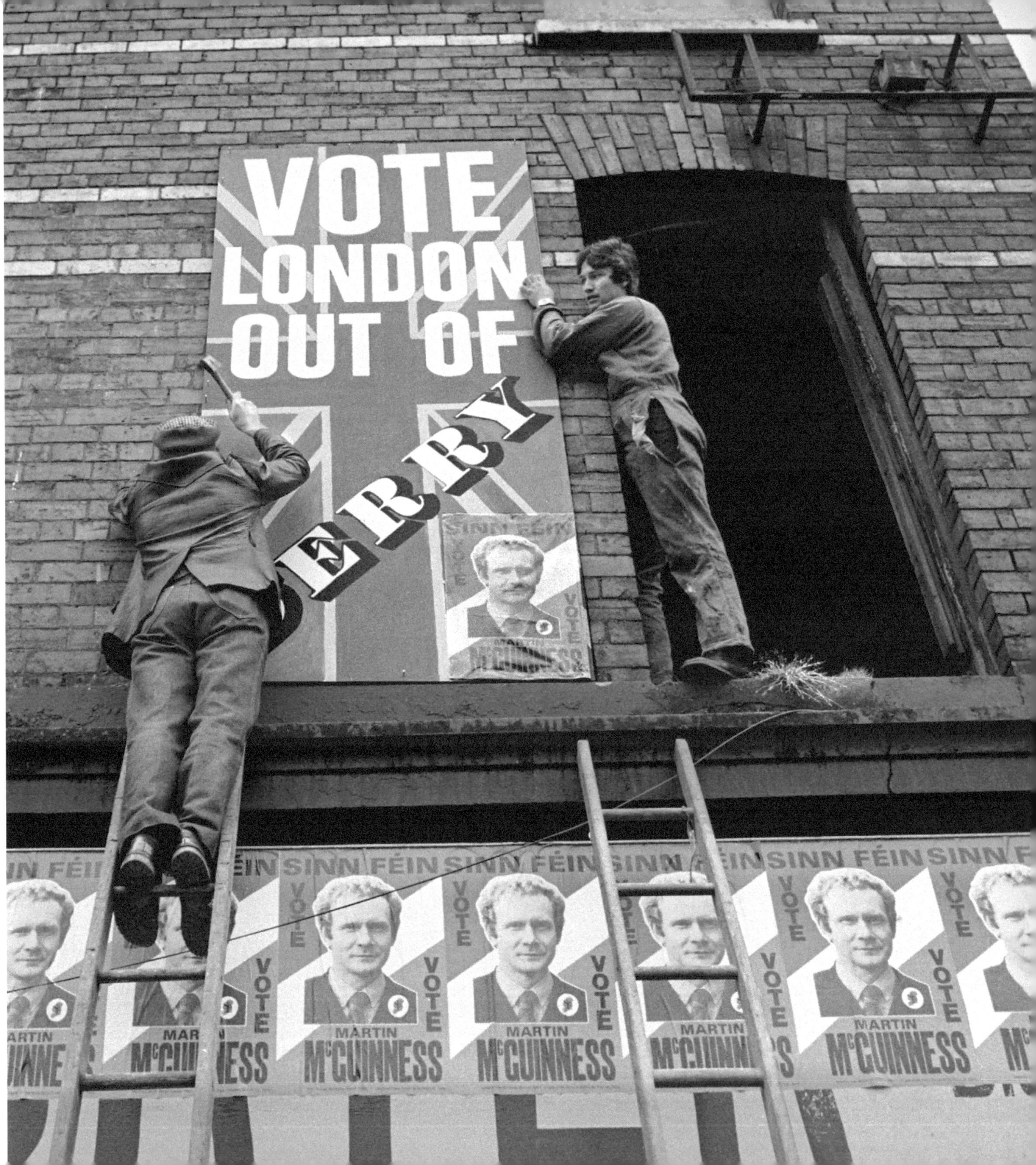

INTRODUCTION *by Stephen O'Connor*

In the fall of 1983, I boarded an Aer Lingus flight to Ireland, where I was to spend a year pursuing a master's degree at University College Dublin (UCD). I'm a nervous flyer. I never believe that a winged machine can pick up hundreds of people and their luggage in Boston and put them down safely in Europe six hours later. I was thankful, therefore, to meet a young couple from my hometown of Lowell, Massachusetts, who didn't appear to be nervous at all. The woman, a slim blonde with a warm smile, wore jeans and a knit pullover. Her companion was a slight figure physically, with longish hair and a Sonny Bono mustache. He introduced her as "Joanie" Ross and himself as Jim Higgins.

I explained my reason for traveling to Ireland and inquired about theirs. Jim said that he was a professional photographer returning to the island to continue a project. He said that though his grandparents had emigrated from Ireland, he had no urge to visit the ancestral home. The year before, he had flown to Glasgow, Scotland, to slay dragons and make stunning photographs. He was kidding about the dragons—long before *Game of Thrones*. But he changed his mind and bought a bus ticket for Cairnryan in the south and took a ferry to Northern Ireland. So began the project that has culminated, so many years later, in the book you hold. The three of us arranged to meet at some point in Dublin, where I would introduce them to some of my Irish relatives.

Looking at these images, I'm struck at the ability that Higgins has of making one feel that the people in his photographs are old acquaintances of his, when, in most cases, they had just met. How is it that these men and women invited him so readily into their world and allowed him to capture some part of their essence and of the reality of their Irish lives? The man with his hand on the tiller while Skellig Michael rises out of the sea to loom over the boat's stern, is concerned only with tide and current and the outboard engine. There is no posing for the Yank in the boat with a lens aimed in his direction.

When the subjects do pose, as in the photograph of the man proudly displaying a pair of greyhounds, the viewer sees the warm radiance of the man's smile as indicative not only of Irish good humor, but of a trust in and comfort with the photographer. Once you get to know Jim Higgins, this is not surprising. He is the very antithesis of the "ugly American." If you want to travel anywhere with a photographer and need to keep a low profile, Higgins is your man. Soft-spoken, unassuming,

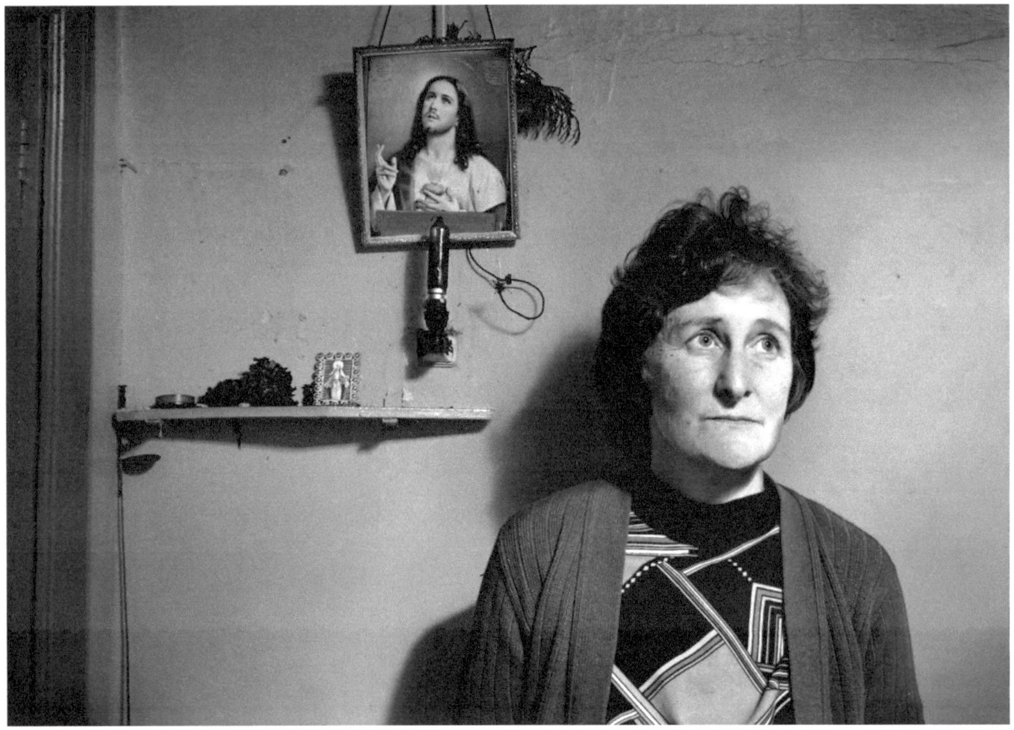

Author's cousin, Betty Grey, Farnaght, County Leitrim, Ireland, 1983

and ever ready to laugh—a quiet, sympathetic sort of laugh—he is someone who can empathize with anyone; someone who makes people feel that he genuinely cares about them, which he does, and is interested in them, which he is. It may be an essential ingredient in his art, but it is not artifice, and one senses this empathy in the photographs of the landscape and the people of this old island the size of Maine.

In his poem "September 1913," William Butler Yeats wrote:

Romantic Ireland's dead and gone
It's with O'Leary in the grave.

And yet, what could have been a more romantic gesture than the hopeless rebellion against British rule three years later, when "Britannia's sons with their long-range guns sailed in from the foggy dew," smashing the resistance, and executing its sixteen leaders. It seems that Yeats had failed to recognize that as a new Ireland comes into being, there is always something left of the older Ireland, even of an ancient Ireland; certainly, vestiges of the ancient nation remain, just as the old stone circles, Celtic crosses, and earthen "fairy mounds" remain, and impinge on the consciousness of modern Irish men and women, reminding them of a buried but very real history. An Irish friend told me recently, "You saw the last of the old Ireland, before it was European, before tax laws made it an appealing spot for investment, before the Celtic Tiger."

Indeed, the change has been considerable. Tom Inglis of *The Irish Times* wrote in 2016:

"The Catholic Church no longer has a monopoly over morality. Everyday life has become more secularised: people no longer operate in the same Catholic time and space. Social relations have become less formal. The rigid protocols that governed relations between parents and children, men and women, and social classes have melted. At the same time, people see and understand themselves as discrete, free, independent individuals who are not bound by the family, community, and religion into which they were born."

Legalized contraception, divorce, gay marriage, and recently the abortion referendum, in the view of many, have finally killed off the old Ireland. The new Ireland, according to Inglis, is "a multinational, cosmopolitan, globalised society."

And so, though much remains, to a great degree the Ireland that Jim Higgins captured in these photos was the last of the old Ireland, a place that my grandparents would have recognized as very similar to the home they had left. I remember my grandfather sternly rejecting the possibility that the great Roger Casement, hanged by the British for treason, could have been "homosexual." "That was all a lie the British invented to discredit him," he assured me. If my grandfather, or even my father, were still alive, they would have found it unimaginable that Leo Varadkar, the current Taoiseach, or prime minister of Ireland, is an openly gay man of Indian descent. The widely viewed video of Varadkar respectfully yet pointedly speaking to Pope Francis about the church's perpetrating and covering up of the sexual abuse scandal in Ireland is another indication that the Irish do not look to the Catholic Church as the final authority on morality, nor are they afraid to challenge that authority.

Higgins' Ireland itinerary was purposeful and exhaustive. From 1982 through 1985, he travelled to Dublin, headed north to Newry and Belfast, and skirted the northern coast, stopping in Derry and Omagh, where a few years later twenty-nine people were to be killed in a bombing carried out by an IRA splinter group. No one was ever convicted.

The photographer's first visit to Northern Ireland came shortly after the death of Bobby Sands and nine other IRA hunger strikers in the Maze Prison. Sands' funeral was attended by 100,000 people. I well remember, even in Dublin, the ubiquitous spray-painted slogan "Smash H-Block," referring to the prison blocks where IRA prisoners were held. One of Higgins' photos captures a child standing in front of the billboard urging Republican-minded residents of Belfast: "Support the Hunger Strikers Don't Let Them Die." In another image, a milkman whose truck advertises "Belfast's Safest Milk," proudly holds a pair of quart bottles while behind him, words on the side of a building remind Belfast's citizens of the ongoing struggle: "H Block Don't Let Them Die." The climate of war is also apparent in the photo of the young man leaning against a wall mural that depicts a Celtic cross backed by the flag of Eire and by An Camchéachta, the Starry Plough, the flag originally used by the Irish Citizen Army, but eventually coming to represent Irish Republicanism in general. Neither is the flag of the country to which he belongs politically, and both represent a refusal to recognize that country.

Higgins' tour continued through wind-swept Donegal and Sligo and from there down to Westport and Clifden. He scaled the sacred heights of Croagh Patrick, then on to Galway, and Doolin, the mecca of Irish musicians, where he found the Russel brothers and their friends cranking out the Irish tunes at one of the frequent music sessions at Gus O'Connor's Pub. He went inland to Tipperary to see the stately ruins known as the Rock of Cashel, or Cashel of the Kings, then back to the coast and out on the sea to the stony tower of Skellig Michael, down to Schull and on to the seaports of Kinsale and Youghal, before heading north for Dublin.

In all these places, Higgins' photographs reveal the essence of both the natural and the urban landscapes. And more particularly, the people—the old man mending his nets, the sexton by an ancient grave with rake and clippers, the broad-chested minstrel in suspenders with a guitar slung over his shoulder, reminding us of another great Irish export, the Kerryman leaning against a great stack of peat he has no doubt cut for winter fuel, the bridge workers in Derry with their soiled jackets and cigarettes, the timid-looking woman by her homemade altar to the Sacred Heart, a true image of the old Ireland if ever there was one.

Higgins always sees the children, too, and nowhere is his empathy more evident: the little girl in her first communion dress, another clutching her doll and a bottle of "medicine for mum" on a barren street, children pushing a younger brother in a pram in Cork, more children playing in the rubble of what one supposes is a bombed-out building in Belfast, and the "tinker" children or "itinerants" by their caravan "outside Dublin," and in many ways outside of Irish society.

While Jim and Joanie traveled, I attended UCD. Seamus Heaney and Thomas Kinsella were guest lecturers. The novelist and poet Seamus Deane taught *Ulysses*. The department head was a gruff old man, the late Dr. Roger McHugh. I remember having tea with Molly O'Connor, an elderly relation, and her friend Nora Harkin, a dignified but frail woman of some eighty years. Nora asked me what I was doing in Ireland. When I told her, she replied that she knew Roger McHugh well. "Oh," I said, "were you in school together?"

"No," she answered, in a matter-of-fact way, "we were in jail together." And for clarification, she added, "During the War for Independence." I later learned that Nora had provided a home for another good friend of hers during the last seven years of his life, the great rebel and writer Peadar O'Donnell. Like many of the friends of Molly and Nora, O'Donnell had fought for Ireland and then gone to fight against Franco in the Spanish Civil War. Members of that bold generation were still alive in Ireland in those days.

I would never change what I did in Ireland nor the people I met. I was able to introduce Jim and Joanie to some of them, notably, George Laffin, a sculptor and painter who restored artwork for the National Gallery, and Molly O'Connor and her family, particularly Dermot and Colm, who kept the pints coming. I learned a lot in those days, yet I can't help feeling it's a pity that I could not have accompanied Jim Higgins in his great circuit of Ireland. There was much to be learned there, too, of Ireland and her people, and of a professional at his craft.

Jim Higgins has continued to grow and discover new artistic vistas, both with Joanie Ross in the highly regarded design company of Higgins and Ross and as an independent photographer and filmmaker. Three previous books feature his documentary images with Joanie's design work: *Fractured Identities: Cambodia's Children of War, Lowell: A Contemporary View,* and *Southeast Asians: A New Beginning in Lowell.*

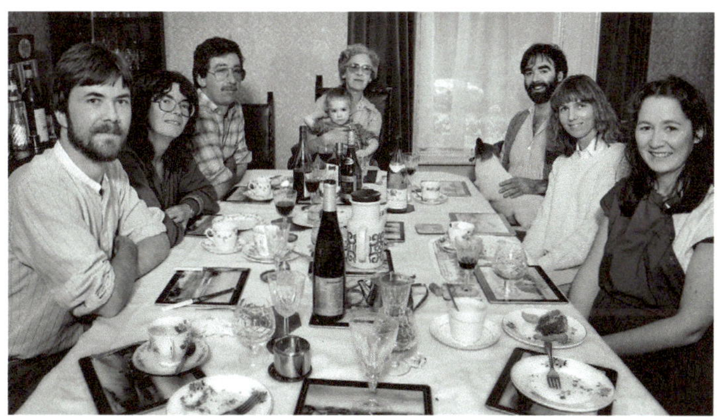

Stephen O'Connor with relatives and friends, Dublin, County Dublin, Ireland, 1984

Jim's signature work chronicling the renaissance of the historic textile mill city of Lowell and the notable settlement in the city of refugees from the Vietnam War and the Khmer Rouge genocide has assured his place among photographers of his generation. More recently, his Flying Orb Productions, a performance troupe and multi-media outfit, has produced visually stunning films that have been shown at festivals throughout the world and in which he employs a cast made up entirely of Southeast Asian actors and dancers. His *Ephemera* won top prize for experimental films in the VSM Film Festival in Hollywood, Calif. *The Kingdom of Kambuja*, a multi-media performance event by Flying Orb, won the Massachusetts Cultural Council's Gold Star Award in 2015. This innovative work was produced with the support of the Theodore Edson Parker Foundation of Boston and University of Massachusetts in Lowell and presented as part of the Children of Refugees program. He has also published *Nether World*, a graphic novel based on the film *Nether World: A Modern Fairy Tale*.

The images from across Ireland are sure to be seen as a distinctive body of work preserving people's experiences in a unique time and place. The people and landscapes we know when we are young often remain forever dear to us. It is impossible for us ever to revisit our youth, or the places we knew as they were. Both are gone. In the photographs in this book, one can glimpse an Ireland that some of us hold in memory. Jim Higgins does not make the case that it was a better place, only that it was a different place, and one that, through these images, speaks to us across the decades of what was.

Author's Note

The photographs in this book were taken between 1982 and 1985. My graphic-design partner, Joan Ross, joined me for the '84 and '85 trips, and we returned to Ireland again in 1988 to work on *The Music Makers*, our film featuring Seamus Connolly and his army of traditional Irish musicians.

At the beginning of this photographic journey, Ireland had one of the poorest economies and highest rates of emigration in Europe. And across the border the Northern Ireland economy was being crippled by ongoing sectarian violence, the British army occupation, and hunger strikes against British Prime Minister Margaret Thatcher's IRA policies.

This all began to change in the mid-1980s with the rise of the "Celtic Tiger," brought about by new economic polices including tax credits given to foreign high-tech companies in exchange for moving production to Ireland. And then later with the Good Friday Agreement of 1998 bringing a peace accord to Northern Ireland. Both sides benefited from the increase in tourism and new business.

This book is a snapshot of life in the Irelands before Good Friday and the Celtic Tiger. Mostly gone now but not forgotten.

The South
BEFORE THE CELTIC TIGER

Remains of Rose Donnelly's house, Farnaght, County Leitrim, Ireland, 1983

After dark Rose would sneak out across the neighboring pasture and beyond the stone walls to meet with her future husband, Patrick Higgins.

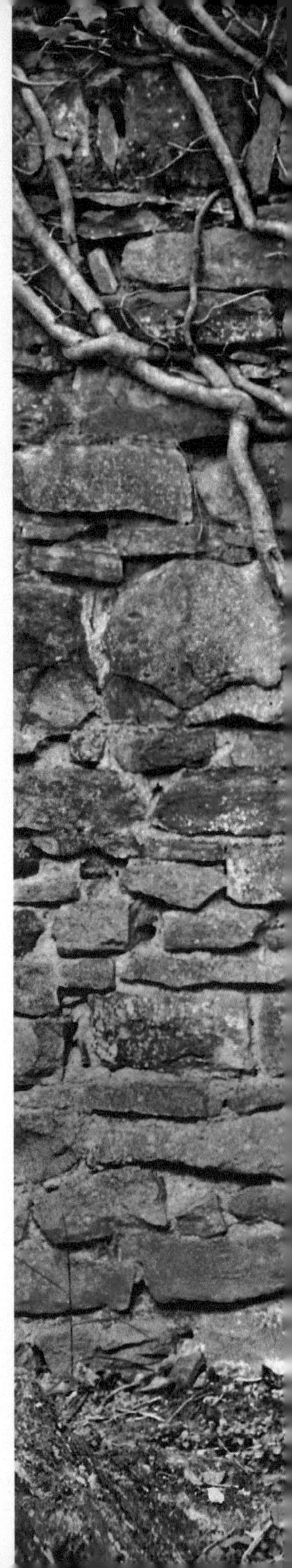

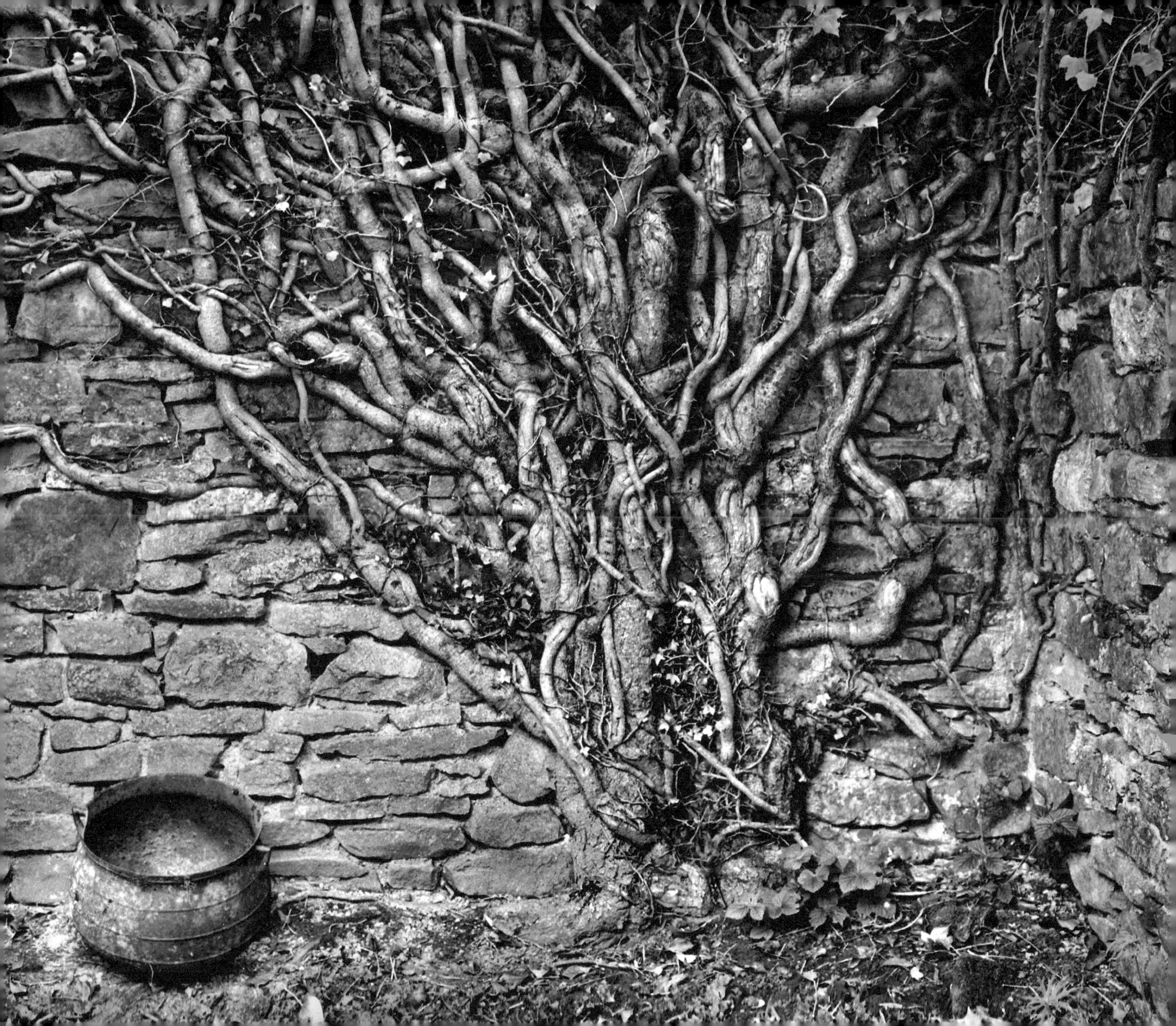

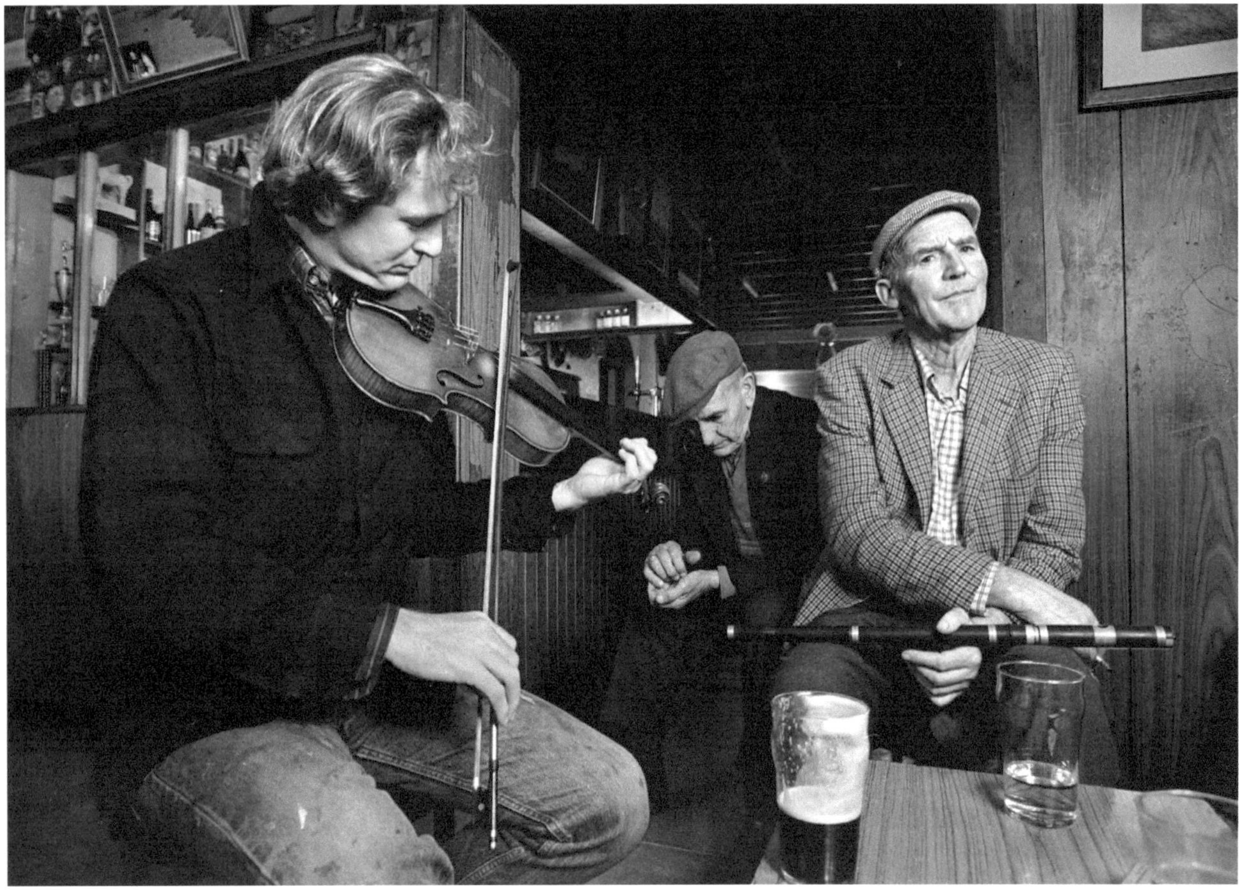

O'Connor's Pub, Doolin, County Clare, Ireland, 1985

A young musician who traveled from Kennebunkport, Maine, to find the roots of traditional Irish music plays for the discerning ear of Gussie Russell (with flute in hand). Gussie and his brothers Micho and Pakie were famous in Ireland and throughout Europe for their unique style of playing.

Village pub, near Lauragh, County Kerry, Ireland, 1982

On Sundays the pubs close from 2 till 4. But if you know your way about, you knock on the back door...

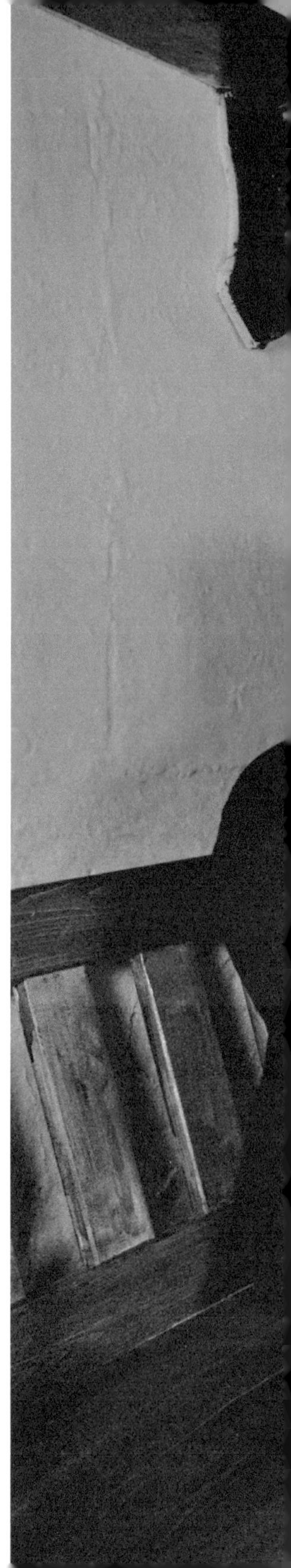

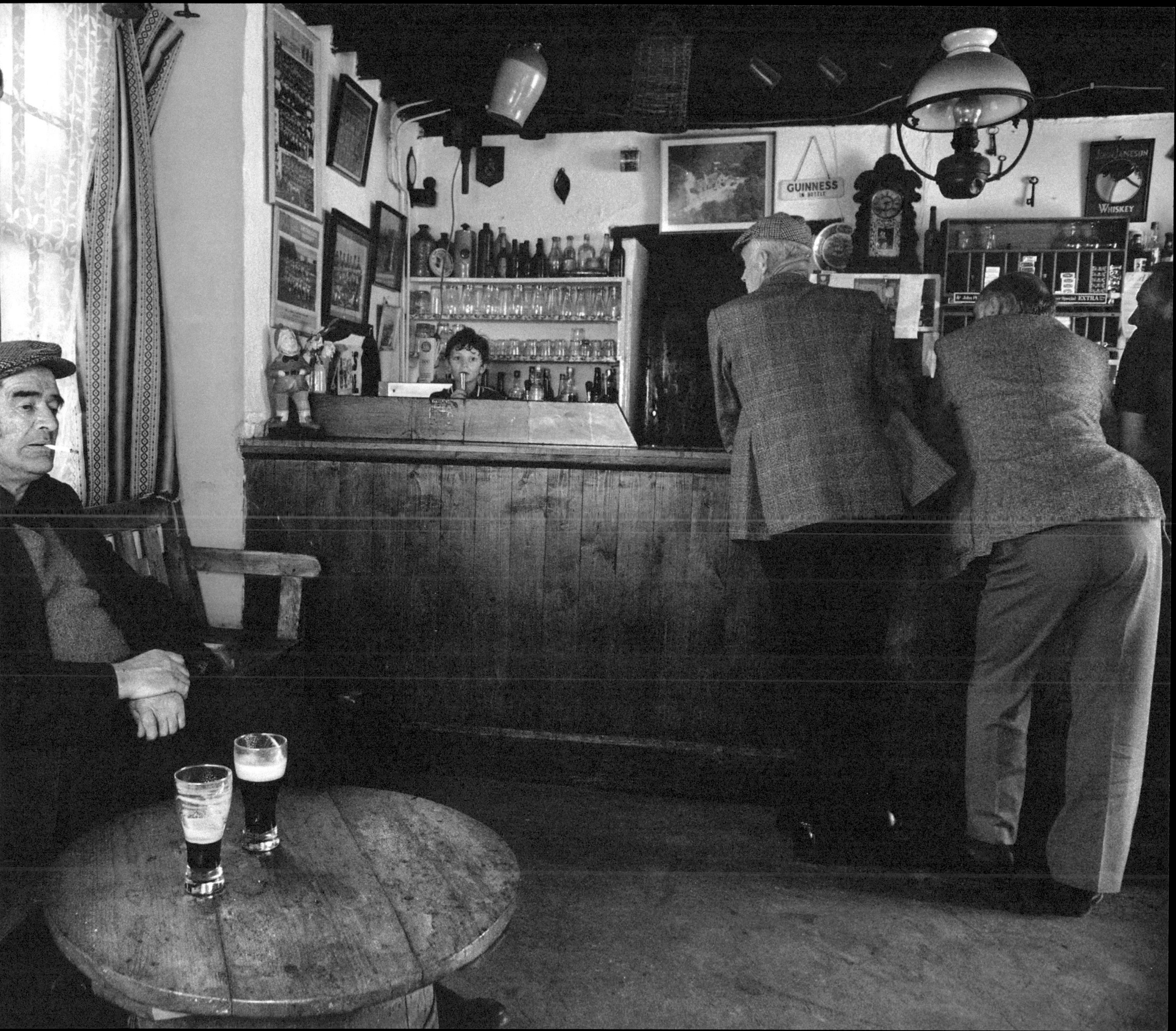
GUINNESS
IN BOTTLE
WHISKEY

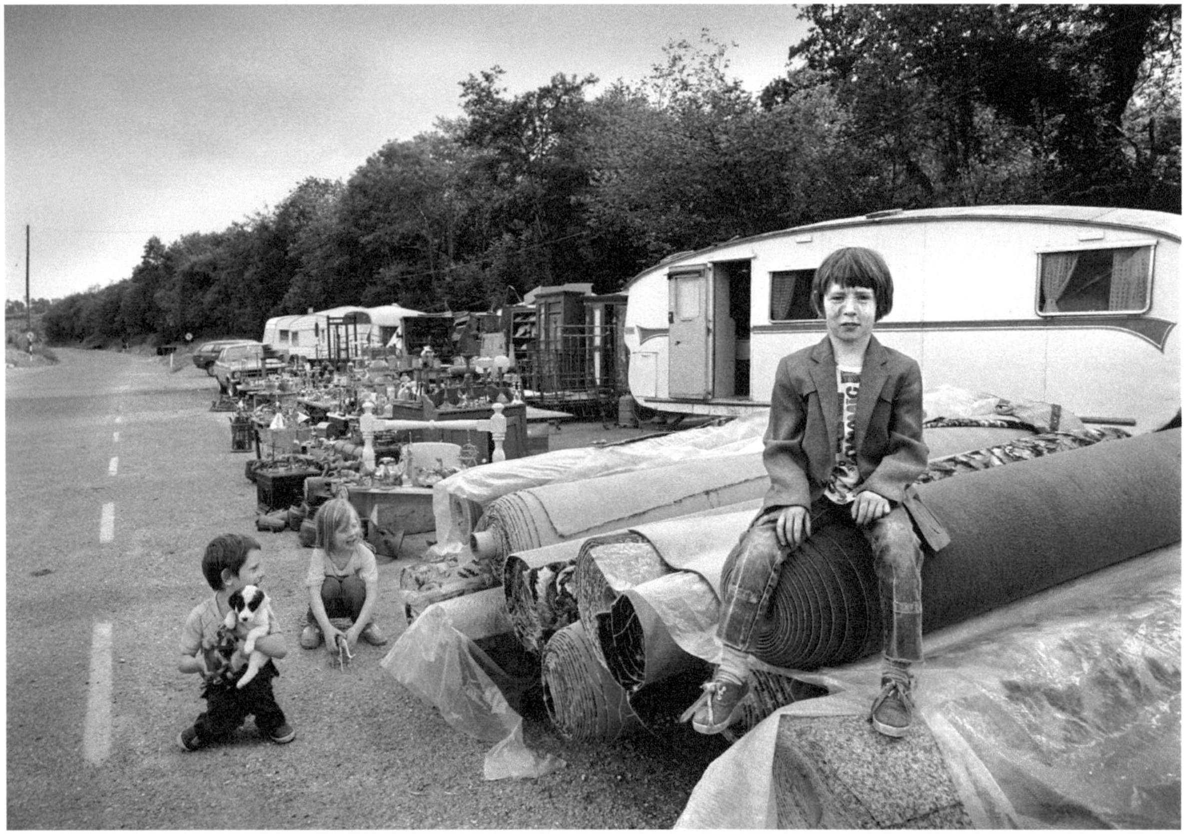

Tinker Caravan, County Cork, Ireland, 1984

Bloody Foreland, County Donegal, Ireland, 1983

The warlord was known as Balor of the Evil Eye. He met his end on the slopes of Cnoc Fola, slain by his own grandson. The blood that flowed from his evil eye stained the hills red, and from this ancient Celtic battle came the Bloody Foreland. Or so the legend goes.

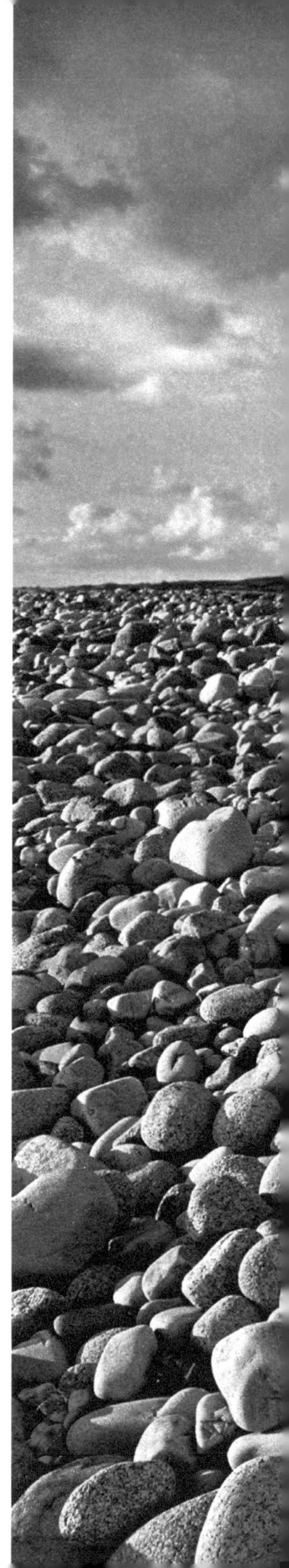

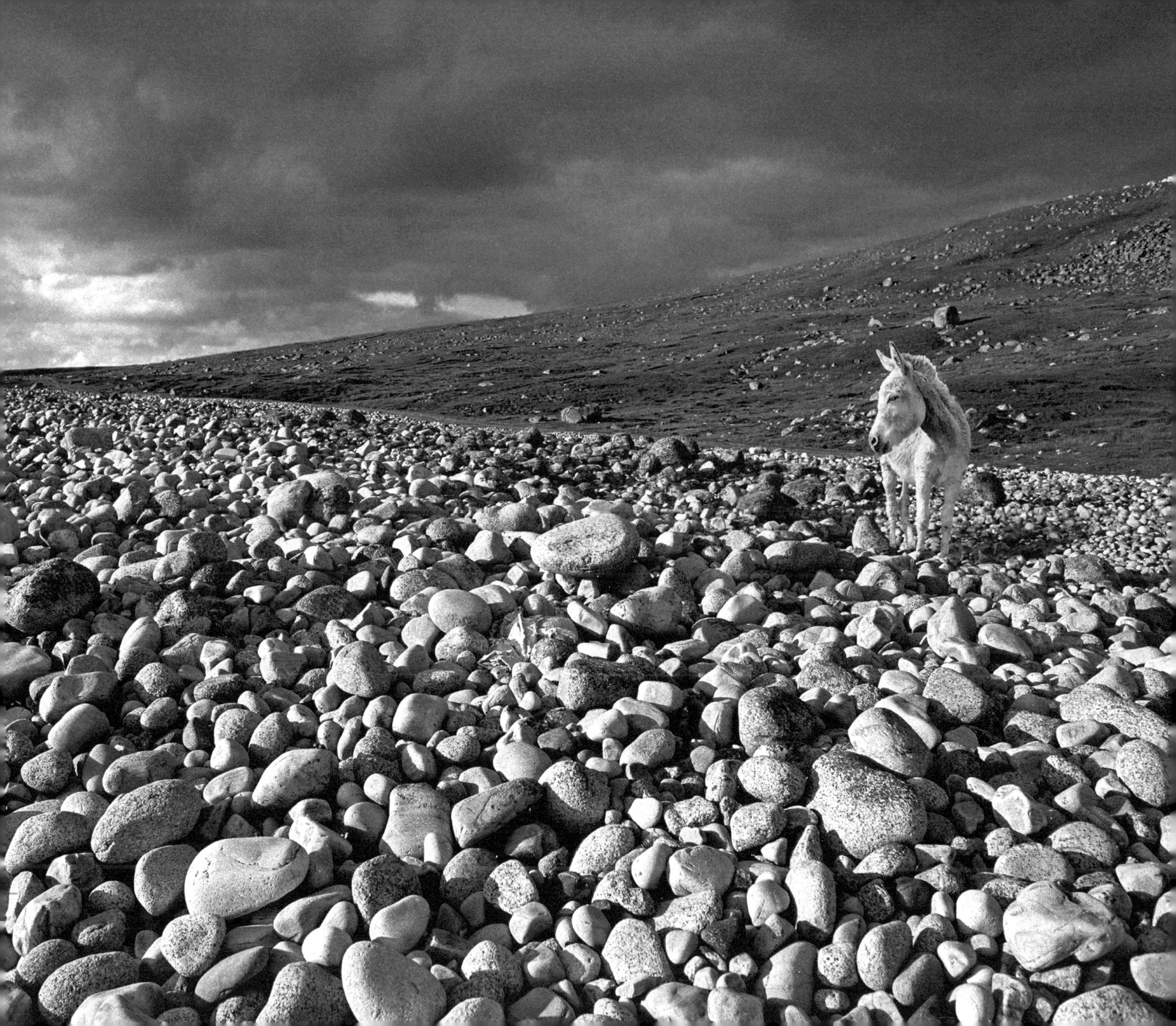

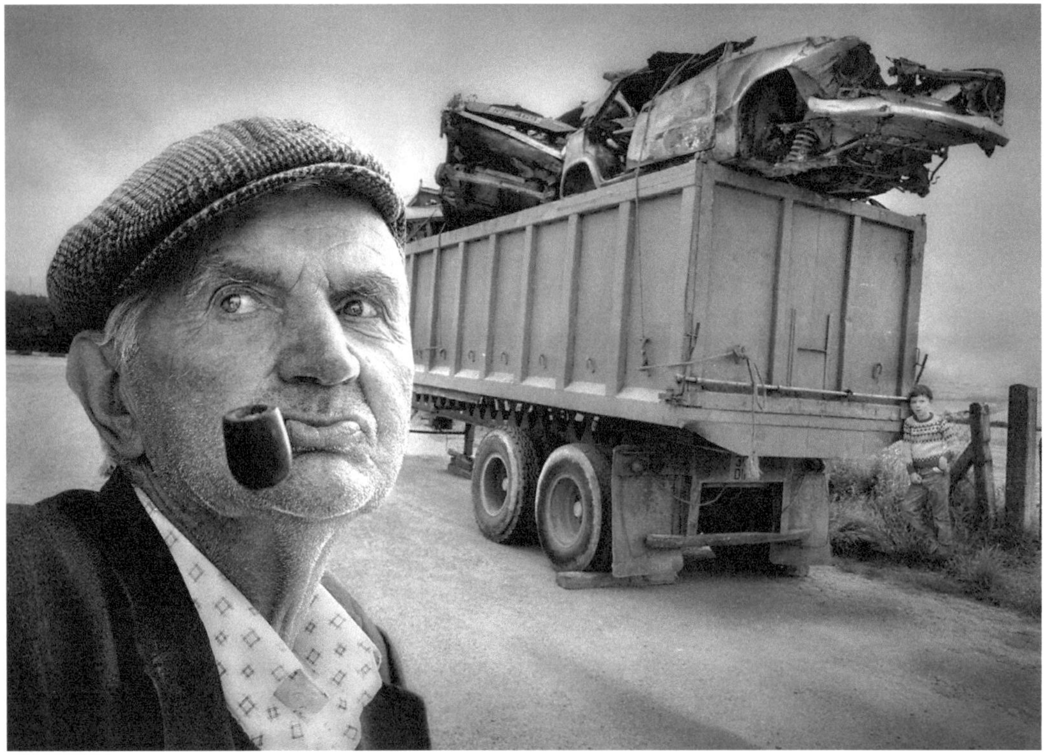

Wrecked cars near Kinsale,
County Cork, Ireland, 1982

Black circles painted on the roads marked fatal crashes.

Landscapes for sale,
South of Drumacoo, County Galway,
Ireland, 1983

Drumacoo
Now look at you
Not half as large
As you used to be
Your arch & apse
Have fallen aside
No longer pointing towards eternity
St. Shorney's well
Fills no fonts
Prayers go unheard
And unsaid
A well kept graveyard
Provides the bridge
Between the living
And the dead
Ghost estates stand nearby
Relics to a new religion
A tiger roared
A bubble burst
And emigration
Took the children

—Peter Burke

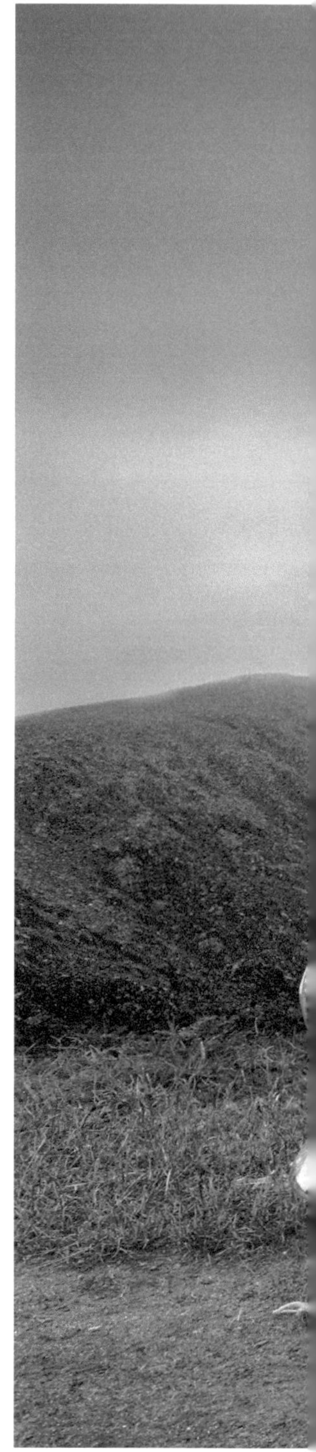

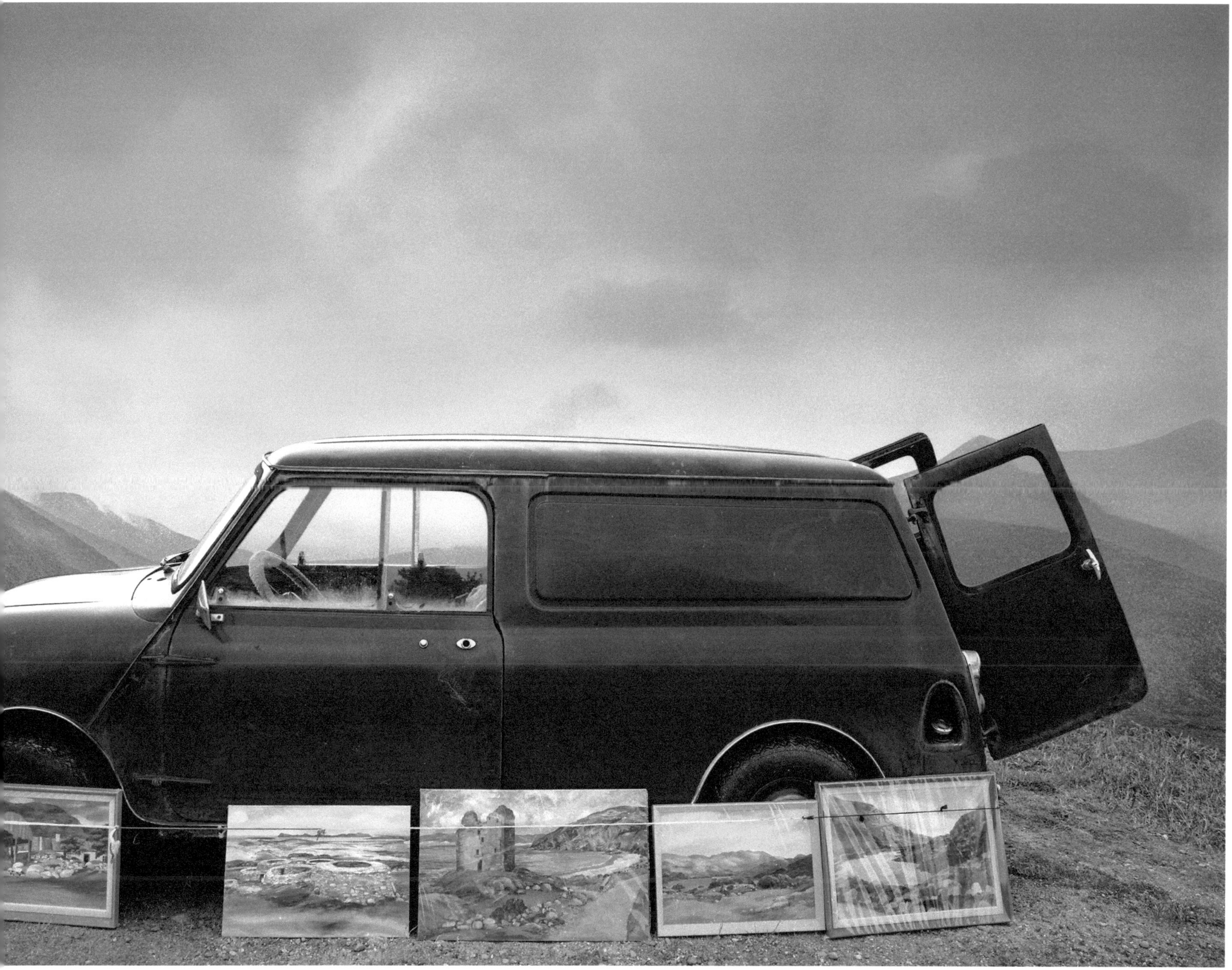

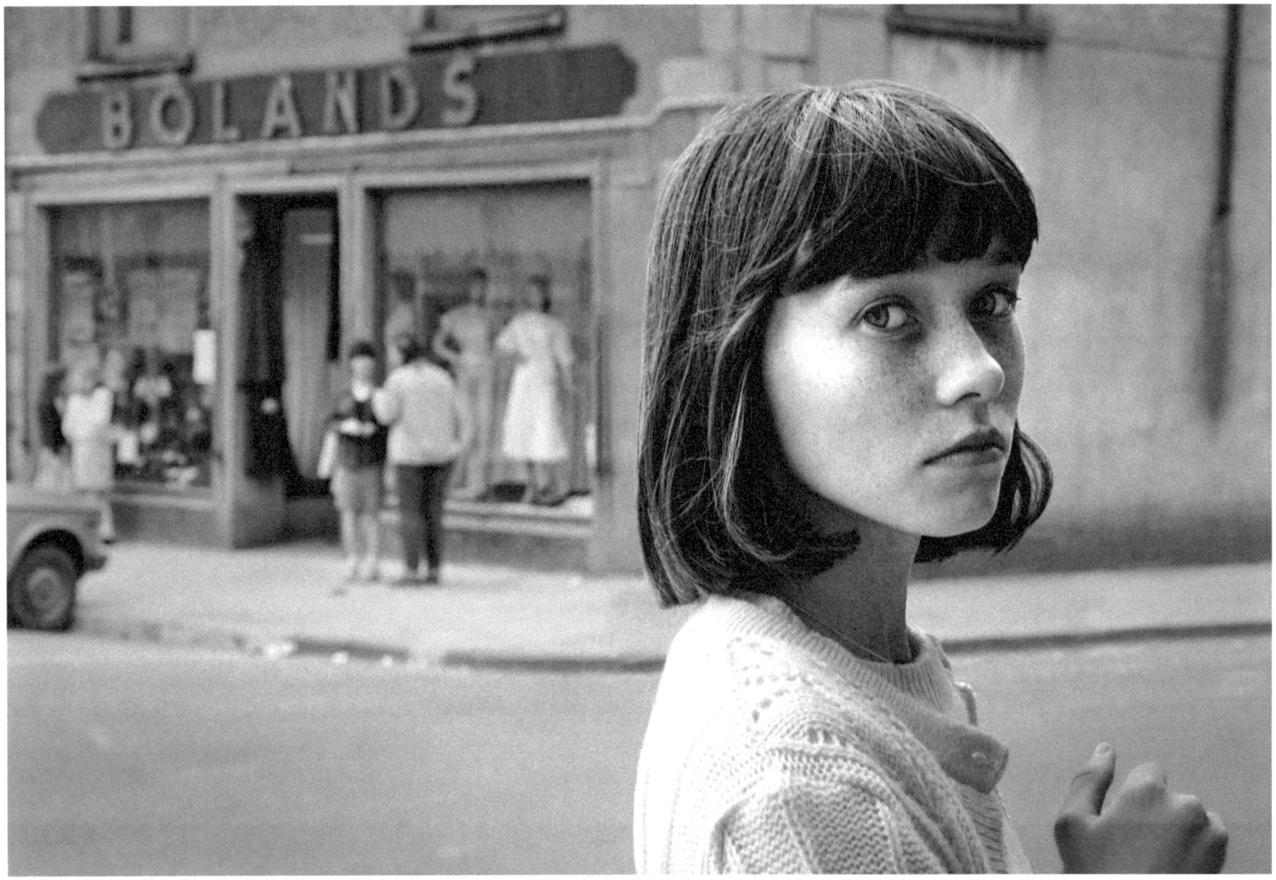

Shopping at Bolands, Swinford,
County Mayo, Ireland, 1983

Racings dogs, Ballinamore,
County Leitrim, Ireland, 198

They were painted on the walls of Egyptian tombs and are revered in Ireland where statues of the most famous racing dogs can be seen in town centers.

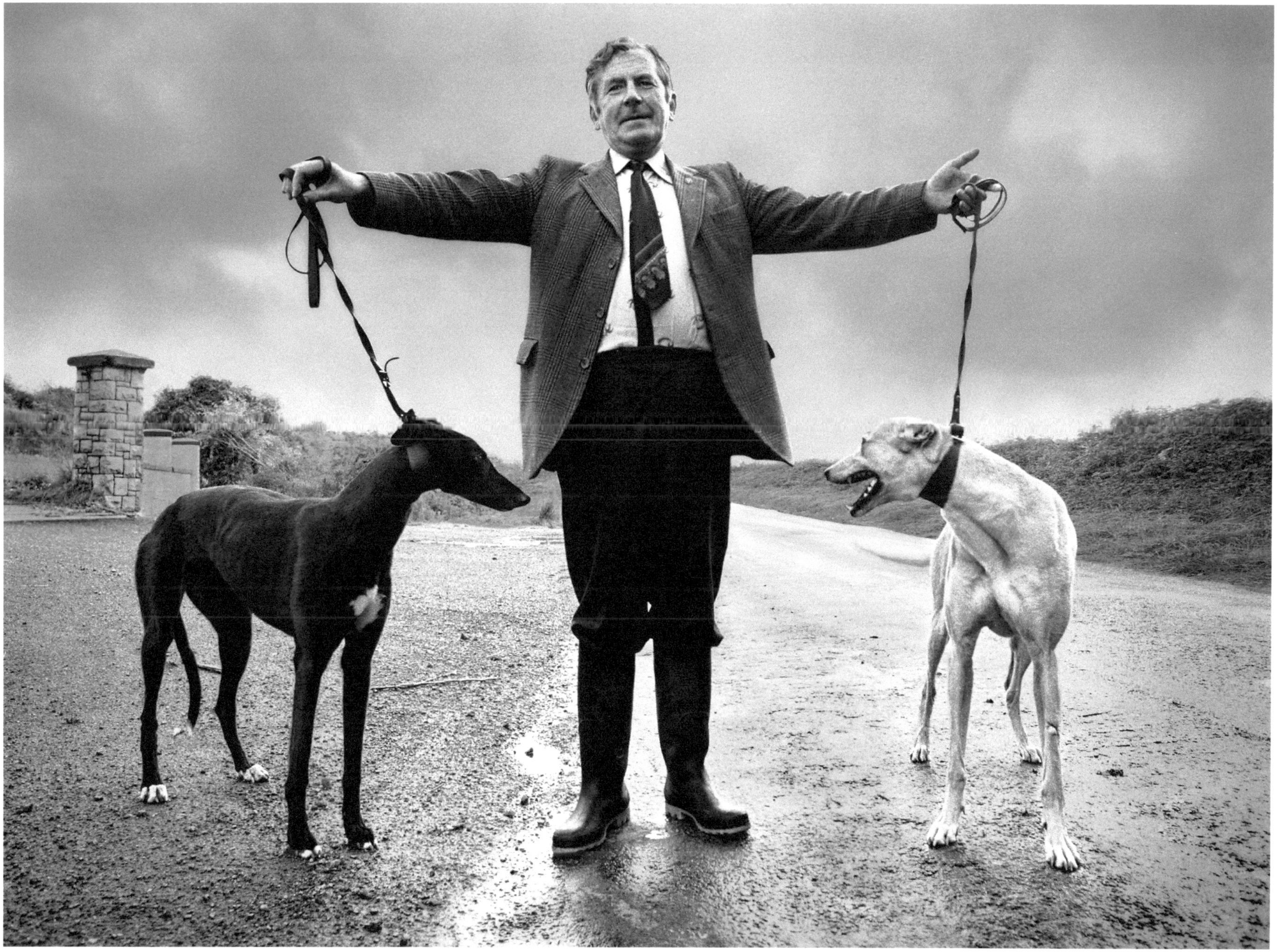

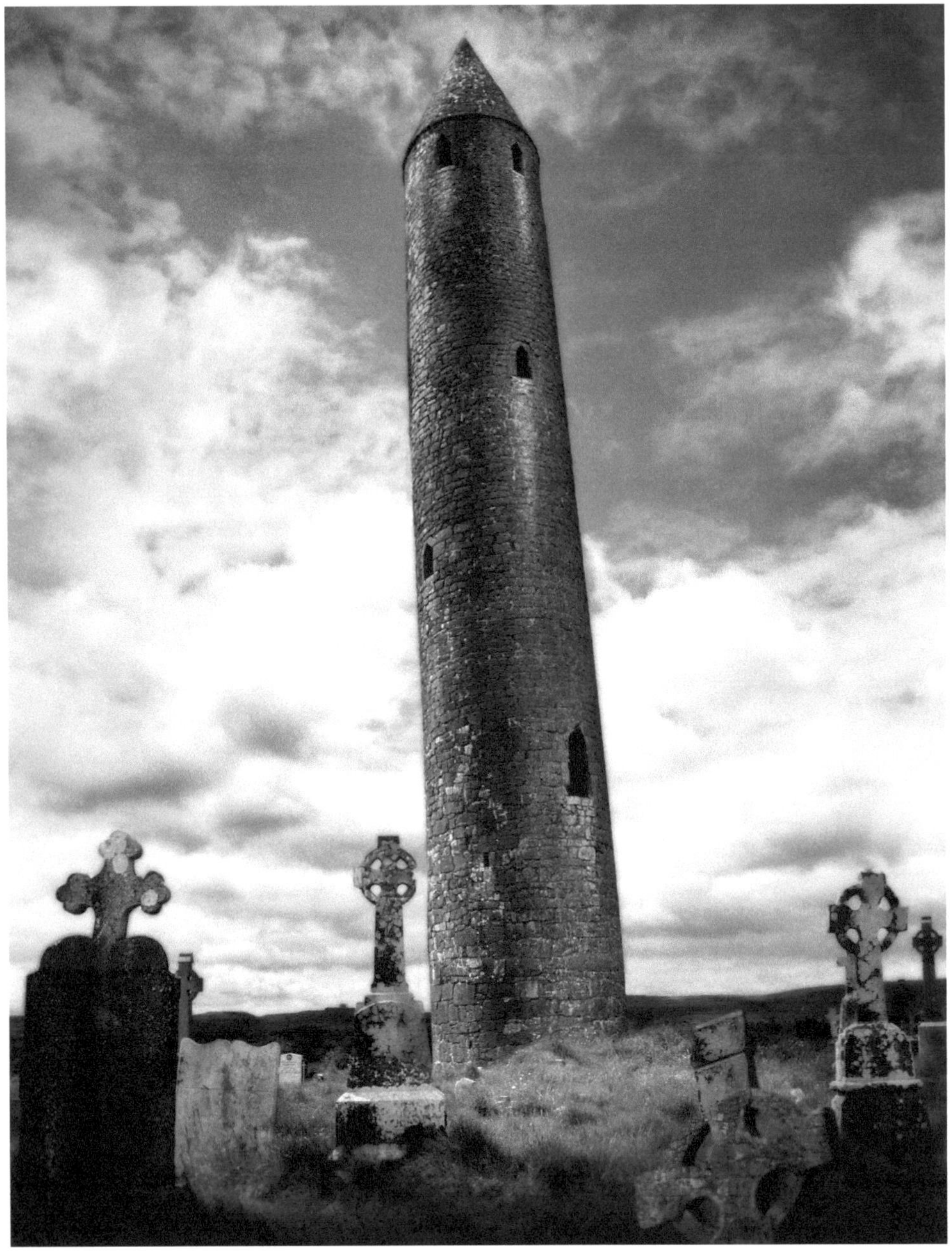

The leaning tower of Kilmacduagh Monastery, near Gort, County Galway, Ireland, 1983

Peat harvest, Portmagee,
County Kerry, Ireland, 1982

Most farm owners on the west coast of Ireland have peat bogs on their land which they cut and sell to the local power station to supplement their small income. School kids would come and help the farmers cut the peat. When the power station closed down, a lot of people were put out of work.

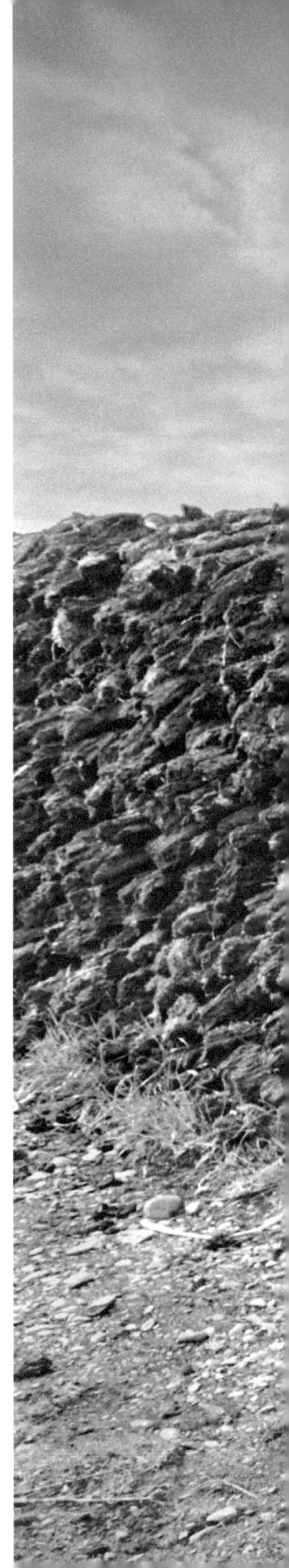

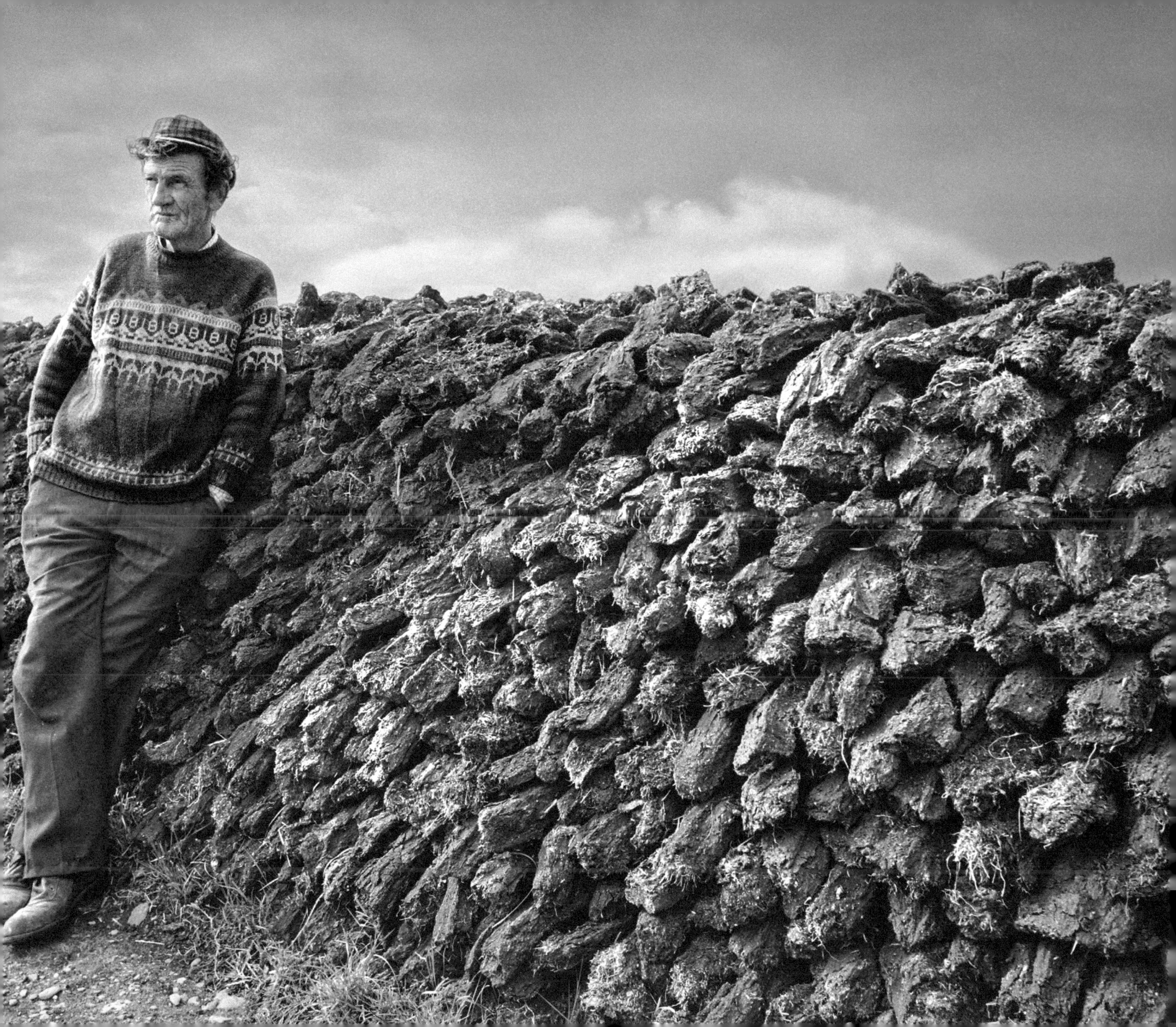

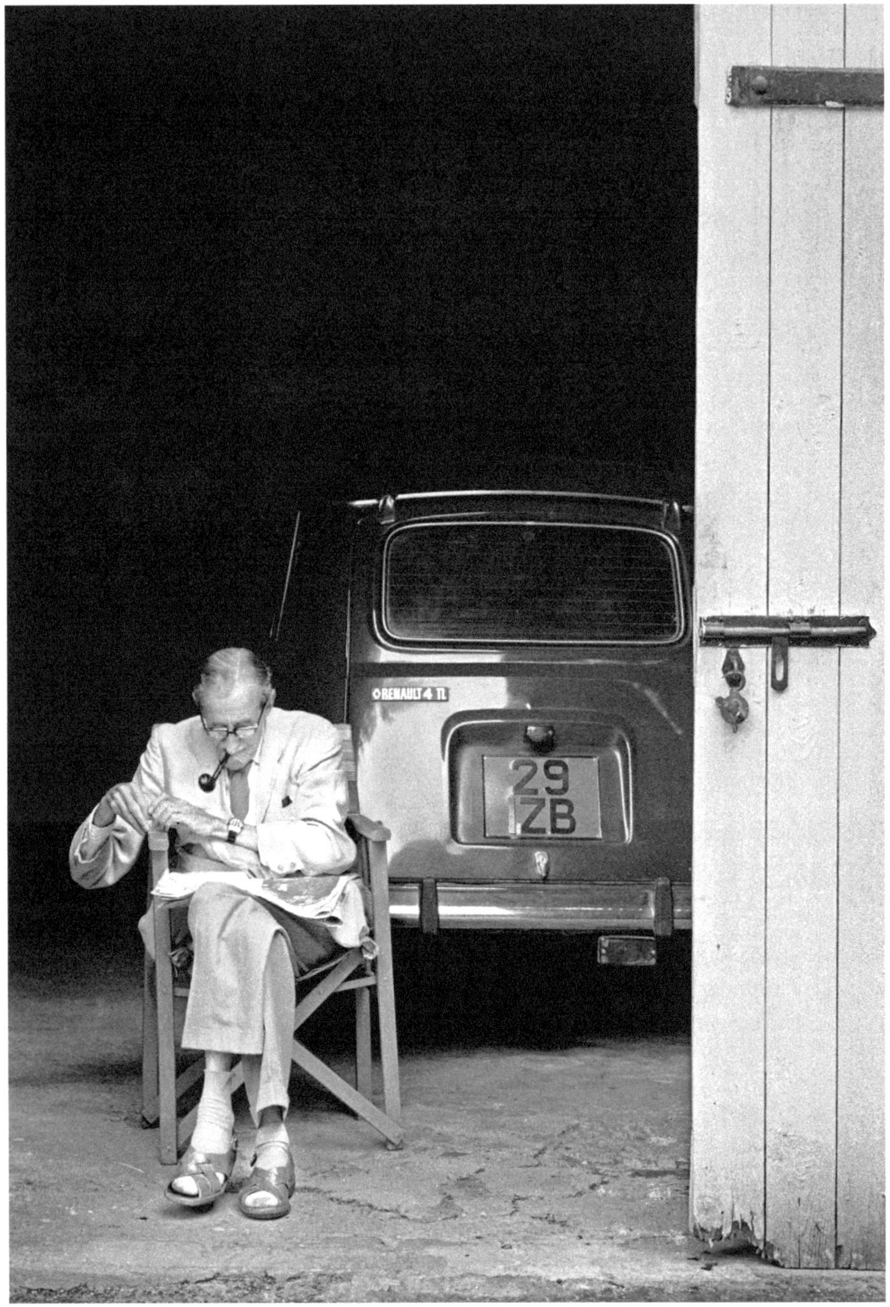

Man with newspaper,
Old Kinsale Head,
County Cork, Ireland, 1985

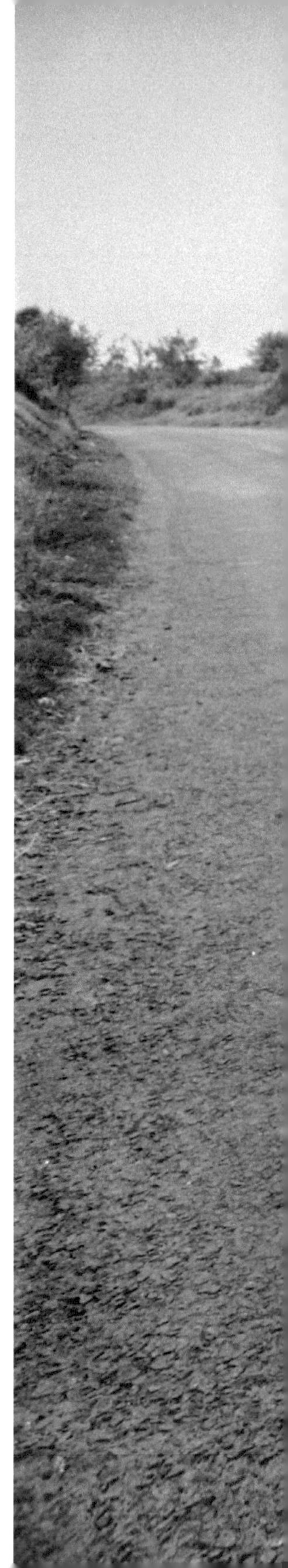

Children with pram,
County Cork, Ireland, 1982

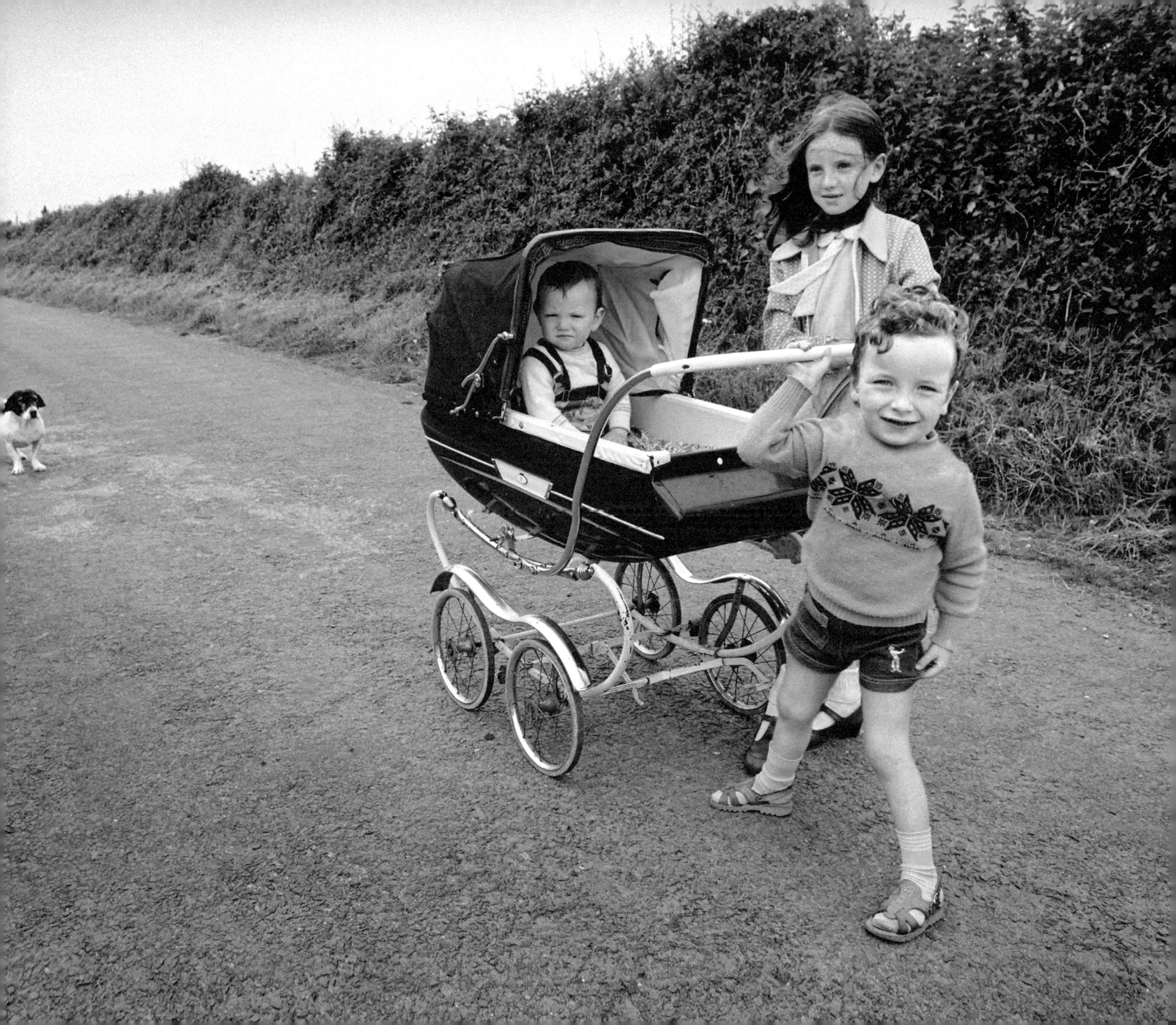

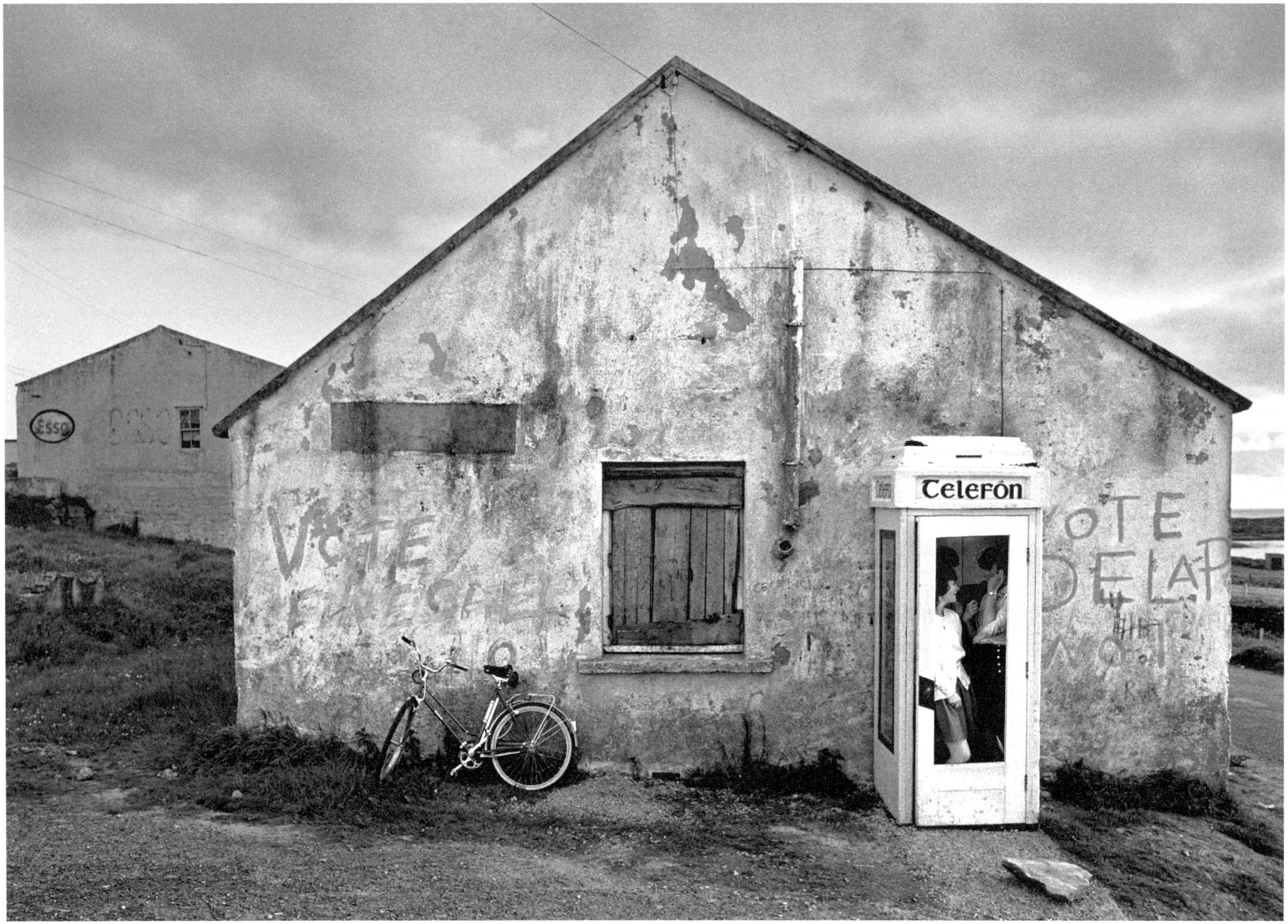

Telefón booth, Glassagh, County Donegal, Ireland, 1982

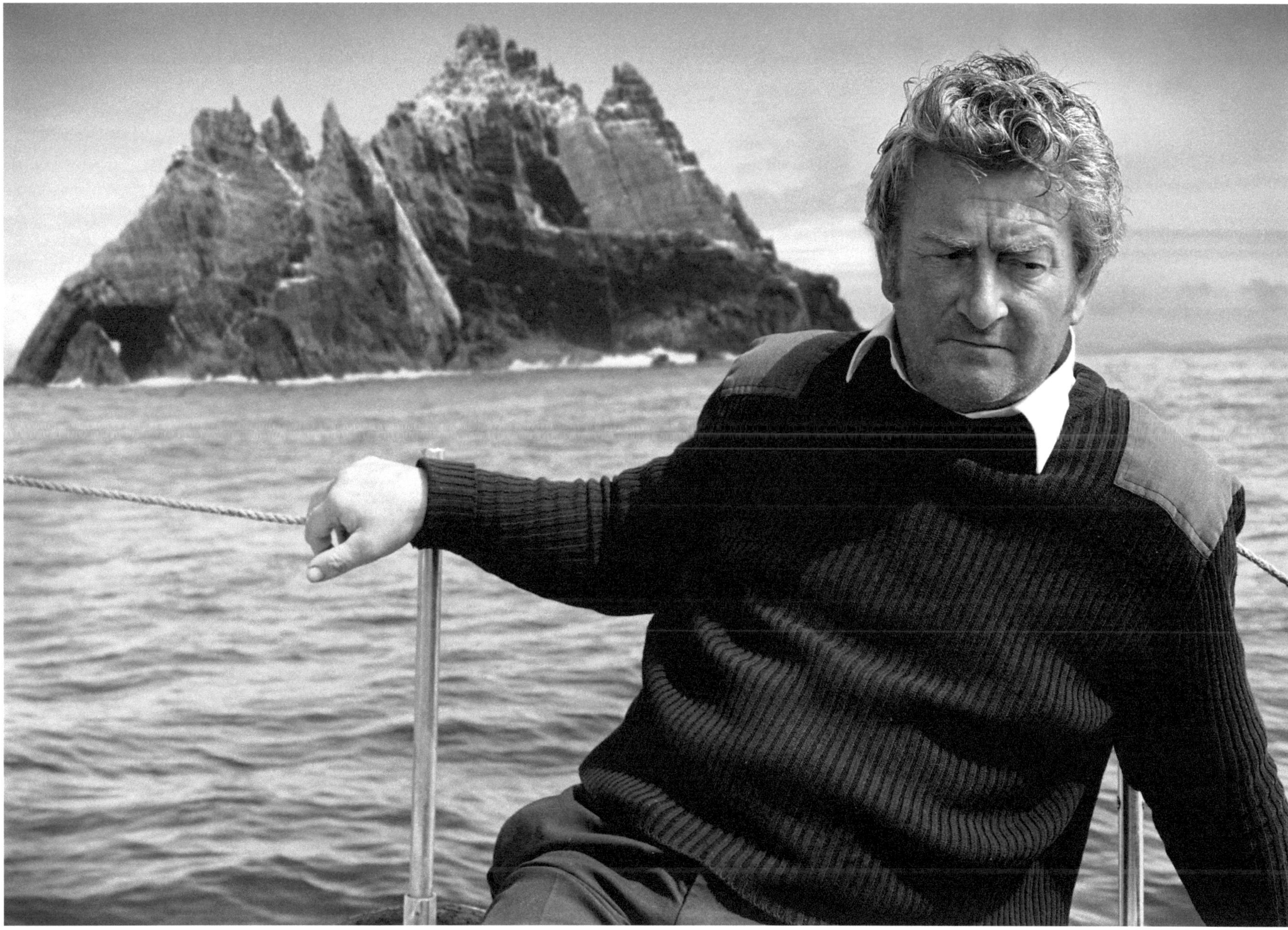

Boat to Skellig Michael, Great Skellig, Ireland, 1983 *For generations, fishermen have been jostled by unseen people believed to have been the dead, but if they carried a fish, no harm would come to them. They mistrusted mermaids and carried holy water to repel them, calling, "In the name of God, be off!"*

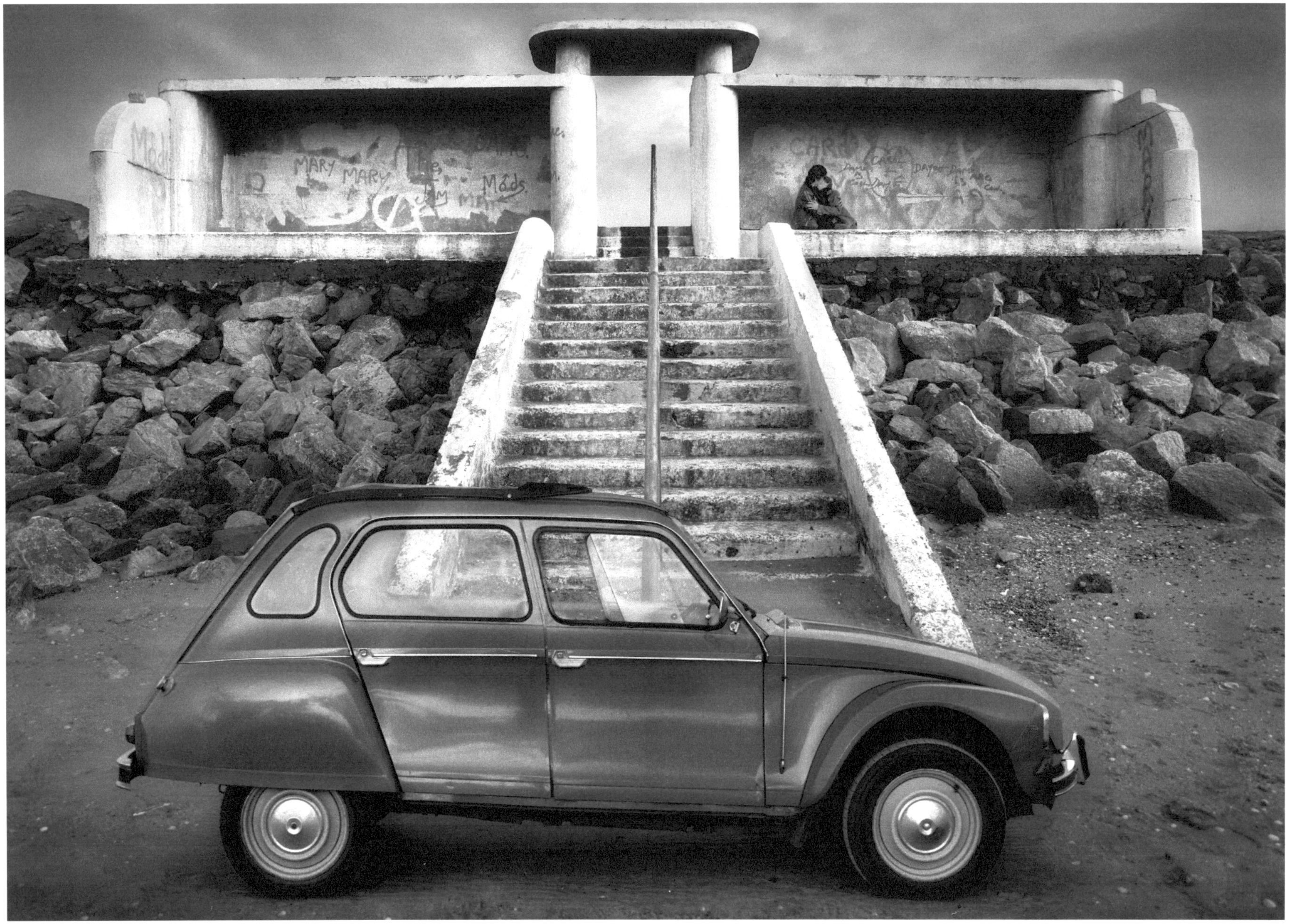

Bathing shelter, Dublin Bay, County Dublin, Ireland, 1983 *Back in the day, bathers were compelled to shelter themselves in a communal bathing box and were supplied with ragged garments called "bathing dresses" at one penny per head.*

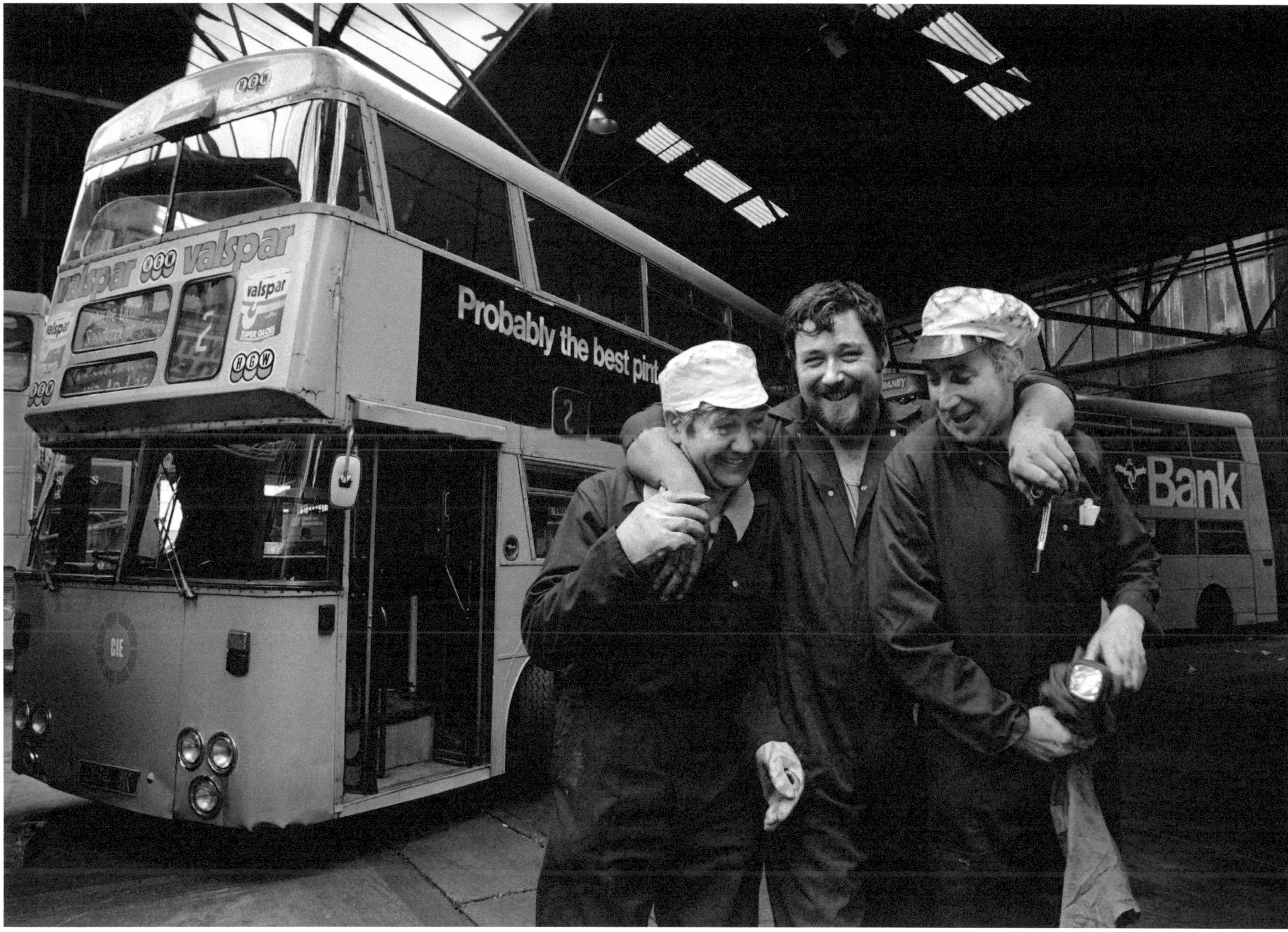

Bus mechanics, Rings End, Dublin, County Dublin, Ireland, 1983

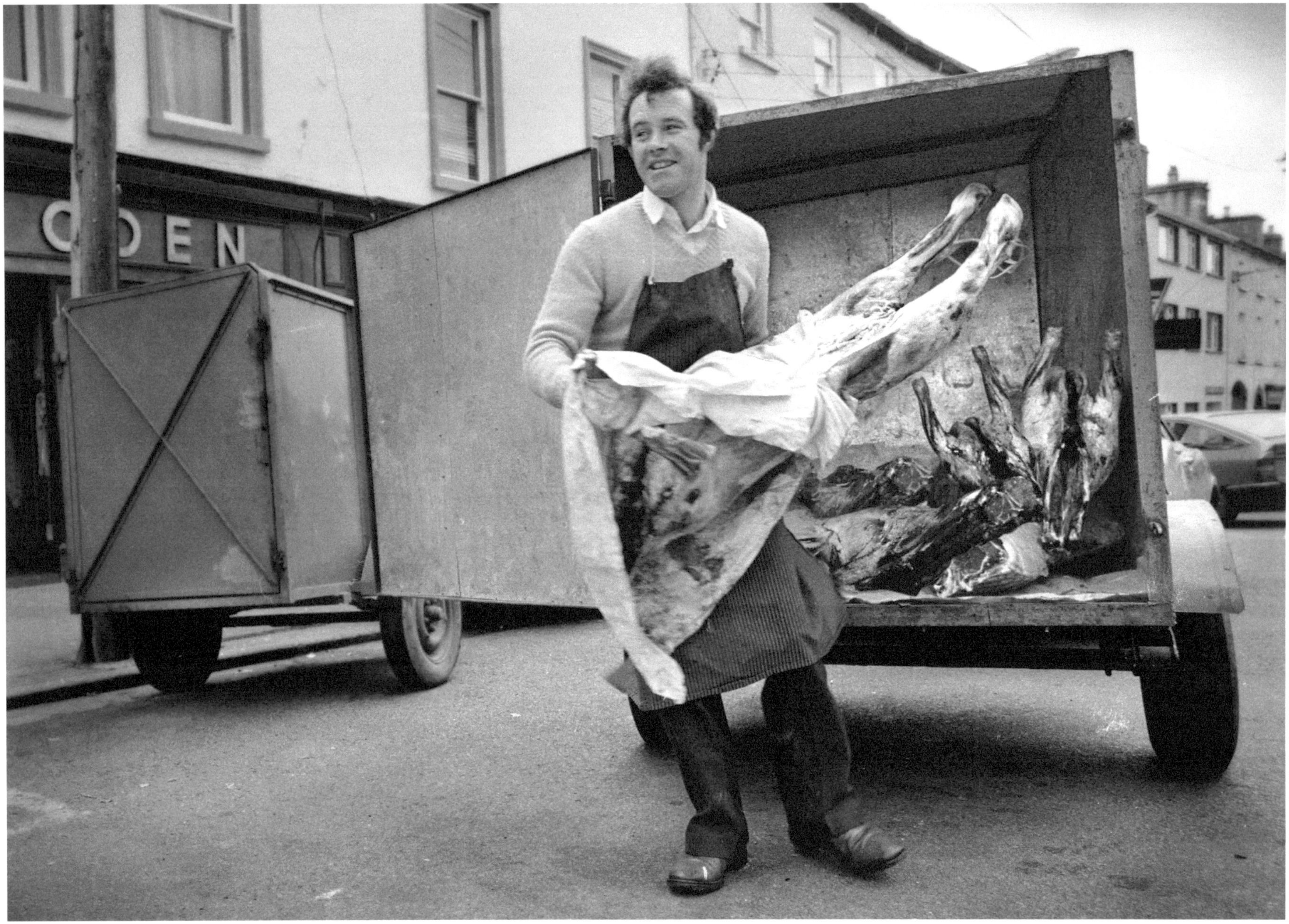

Meat wagon, Killorglin, County Kerry, Ireland, 1982

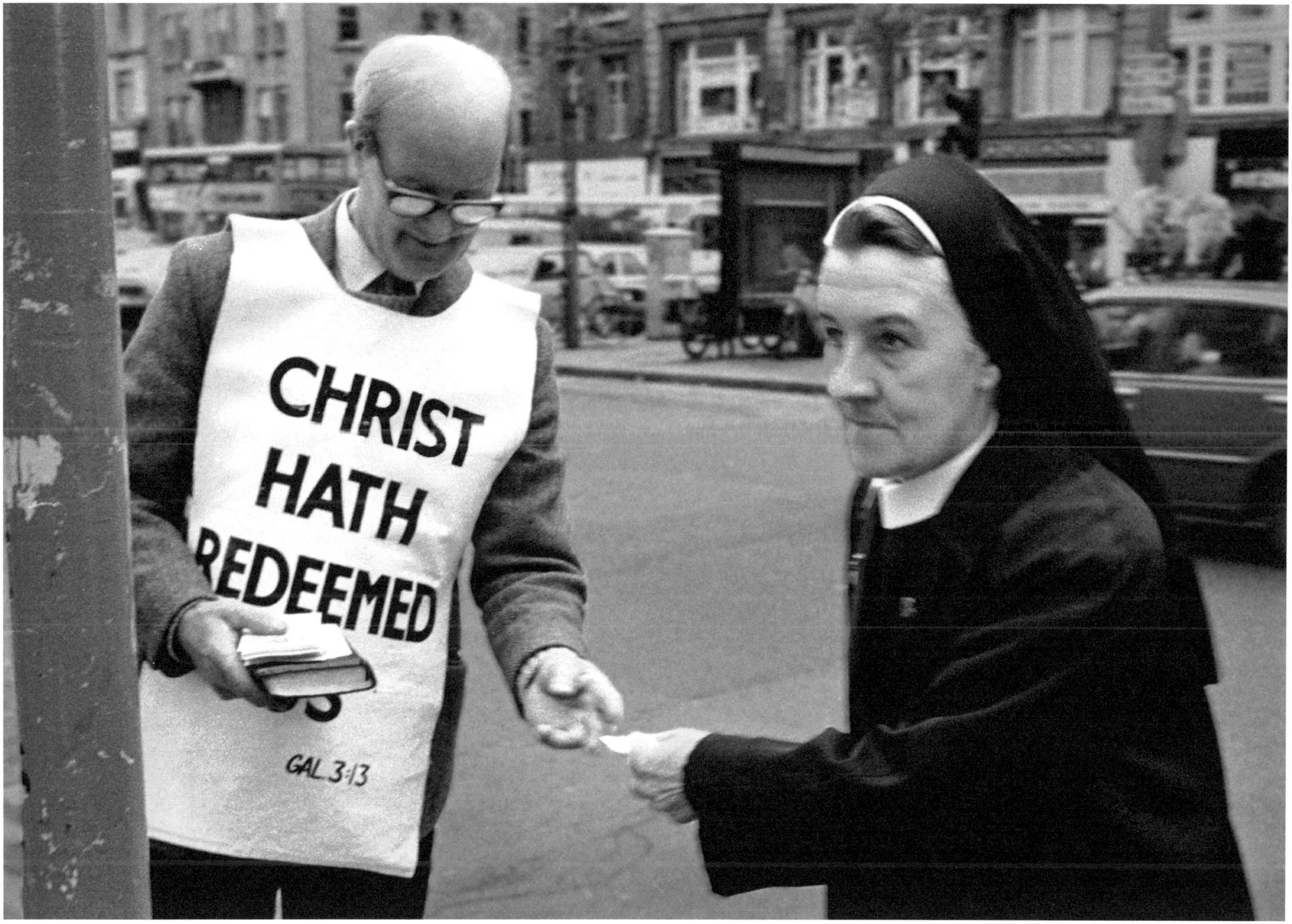

“Christ Hath Redeemed,” Tralee, County Kerry, Ireland, 1982

Burial ground, Rock of Cashel, County Tipperary, Ireland, 1984

"I wash the stone with a caustic soda, then come back the next day with a wire brush and rub it down. My parents are buried here along with my grandparents, great uncle, and first cousin."

—Richard Luby

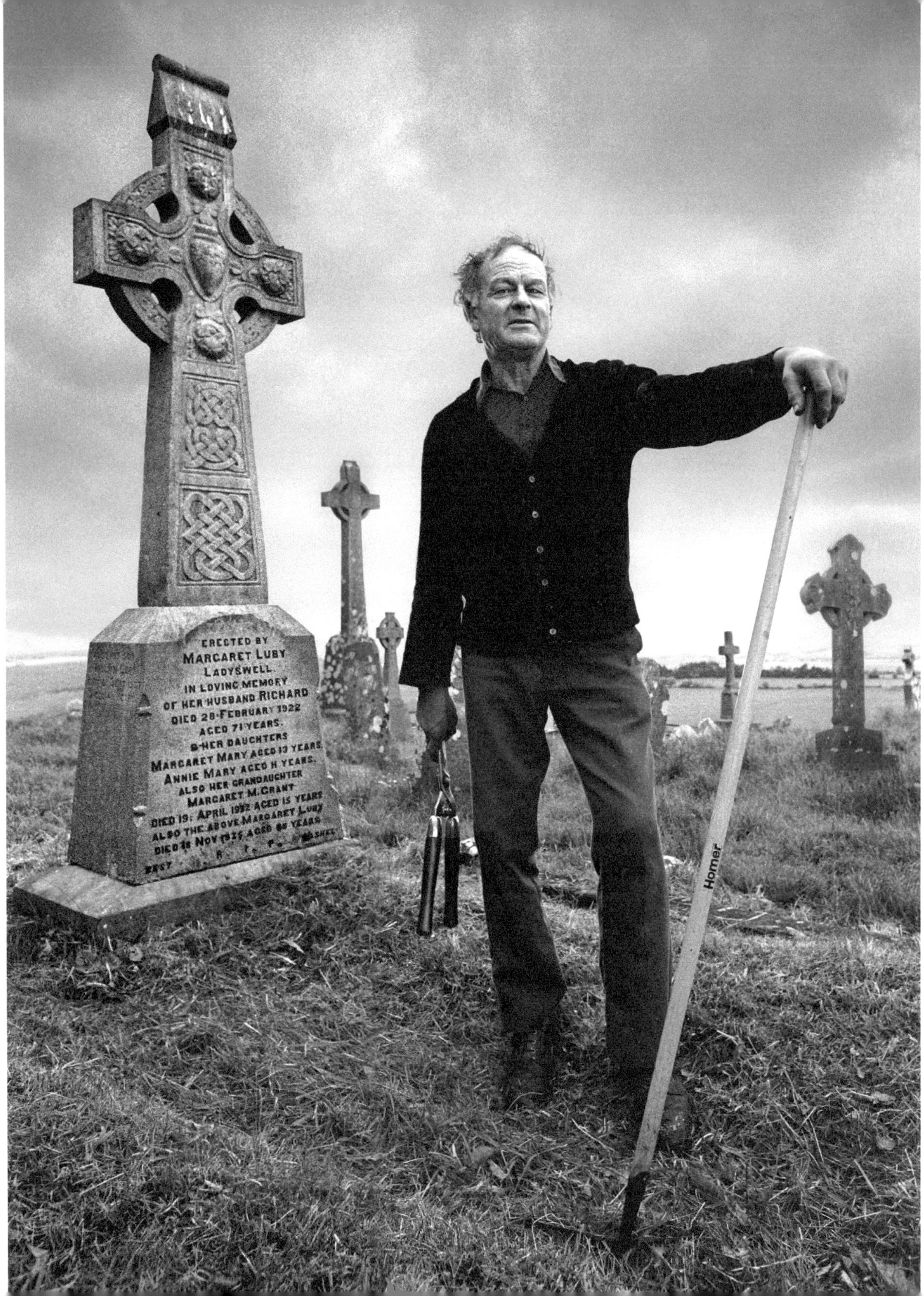

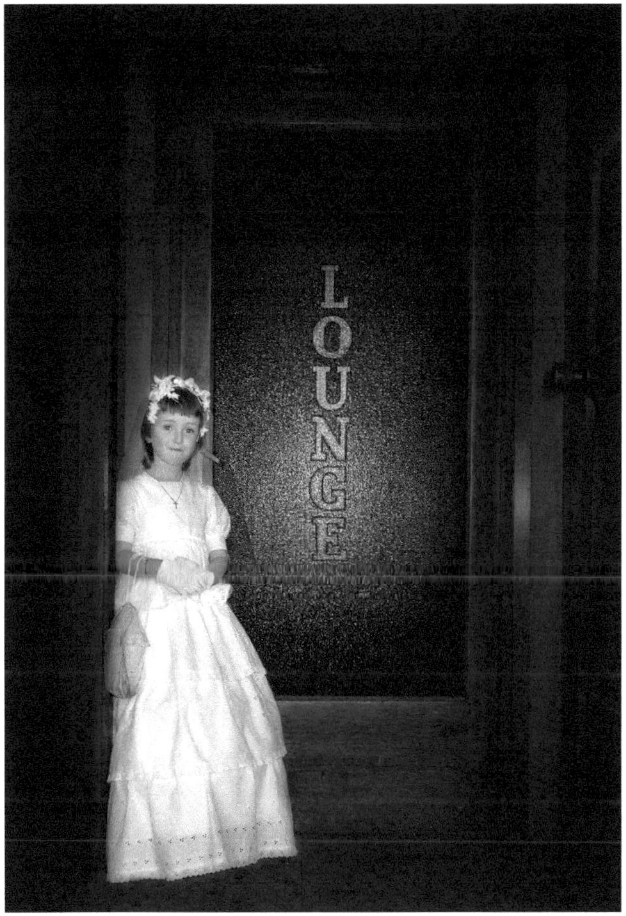

First Holy Communion, Charlestown,
County Mayo, Ireland, 1983

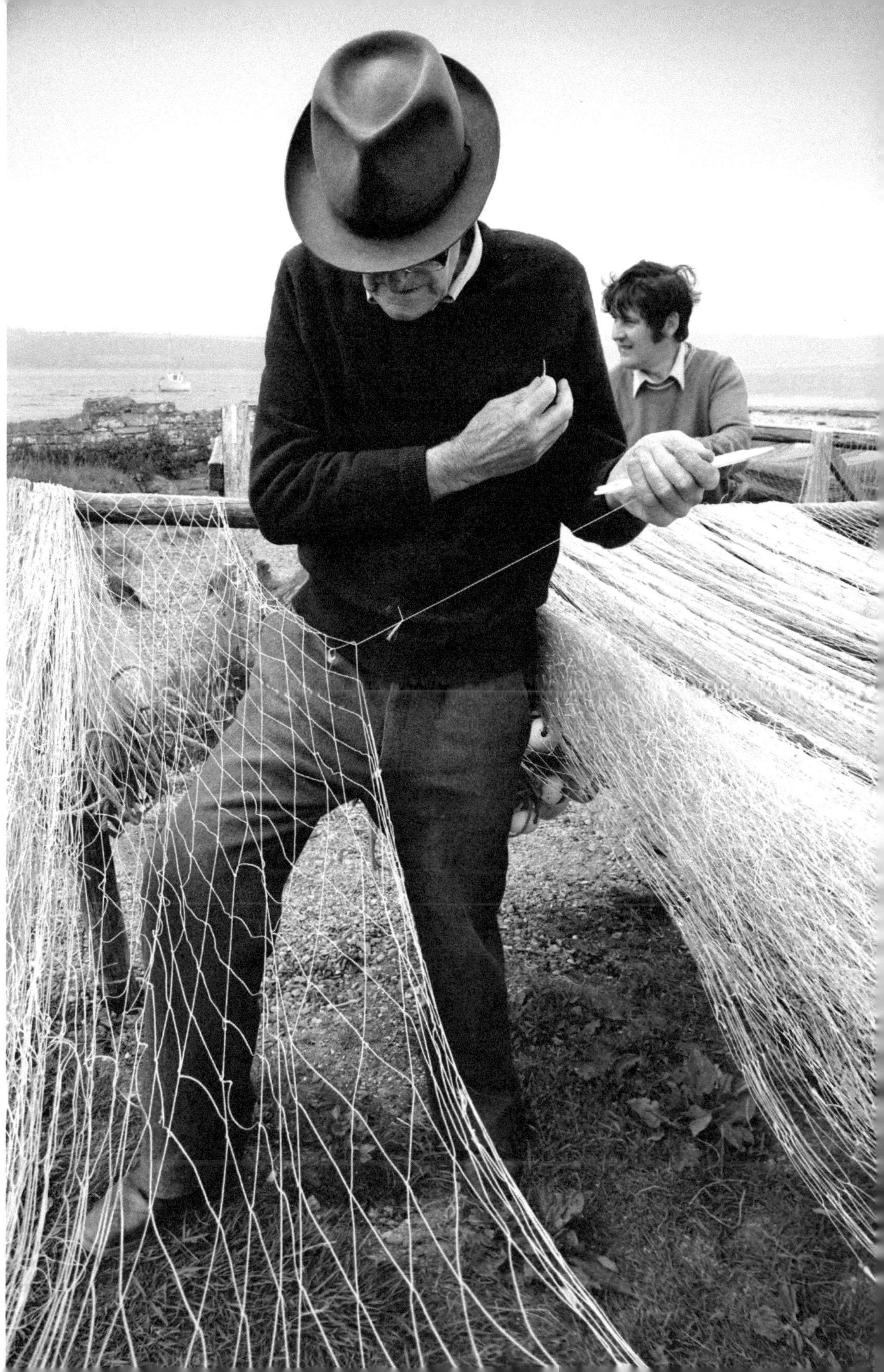

Fishermen mending nets, Clifden,
County Galway, Ireland, 1983

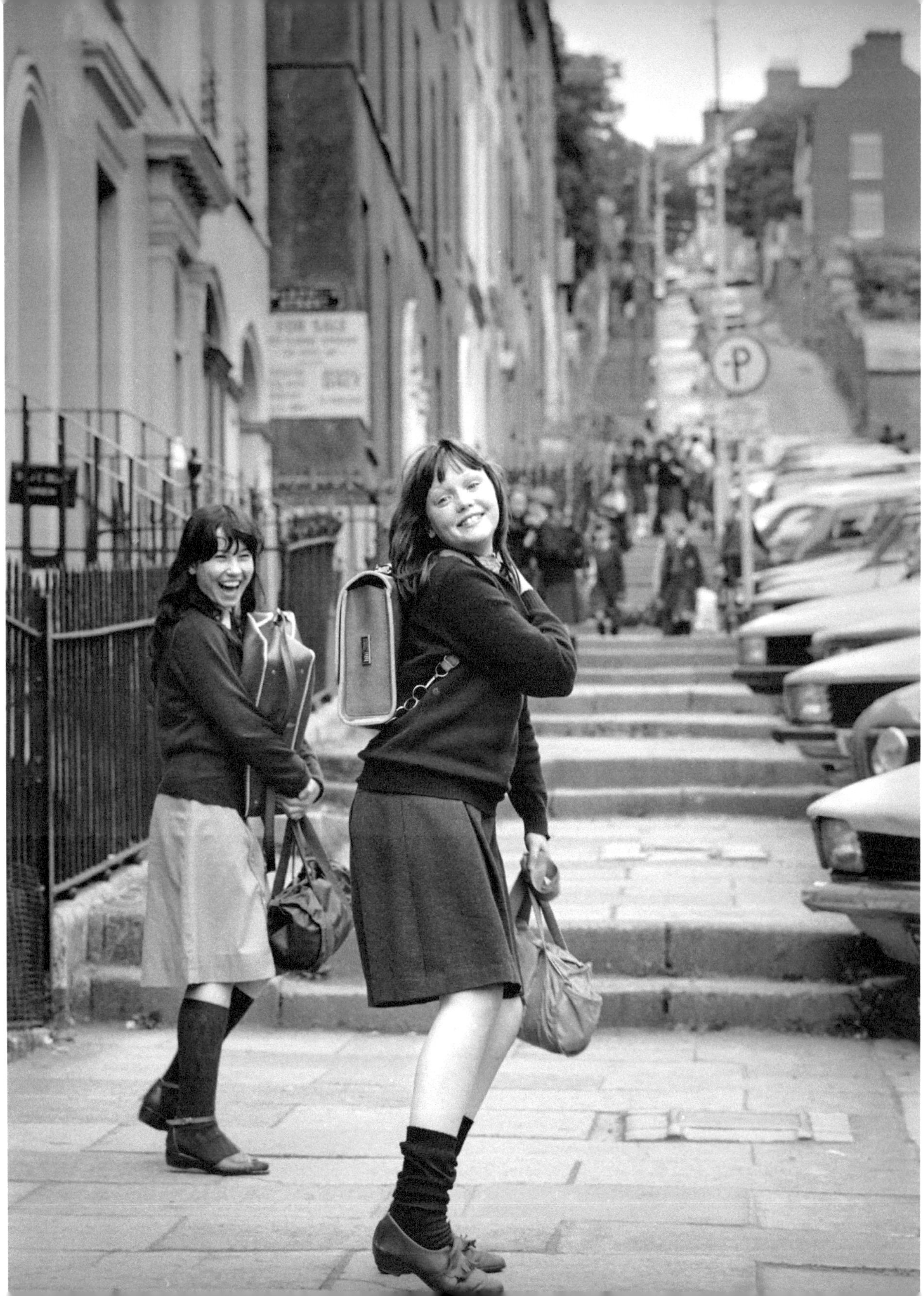

Catholic school girls,
Cork City, County Cork,
Ireland, 1983

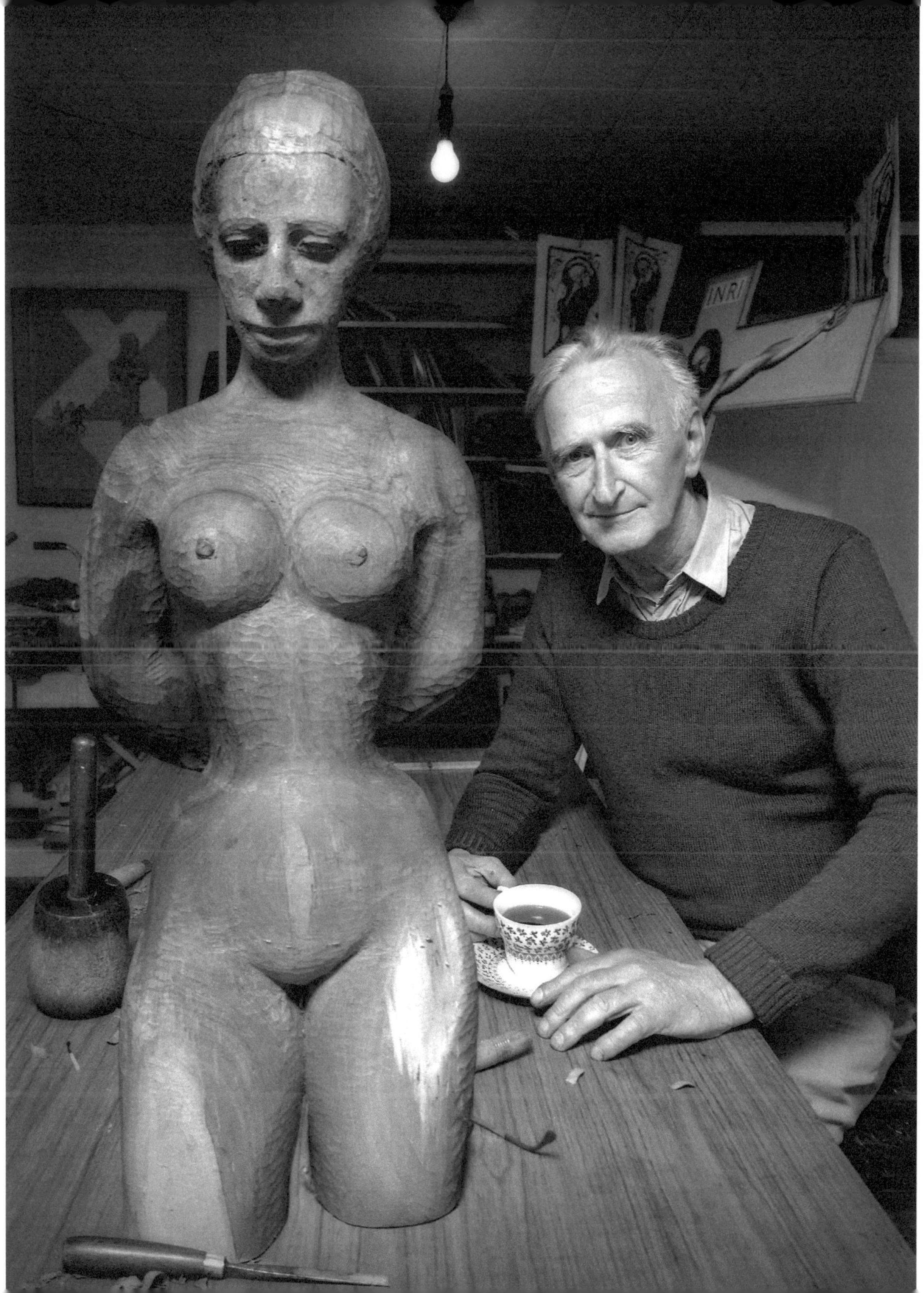

Sculptor, Dublin,
County Dublin, Ireland, 1984

Writers, poets, composers, sculptors, painters, and other artists pay no taxes on the sale of their work. This law was instituted by the government in 1969 to encourage artists to work and stay in Ireland.

—George Barry Laffan

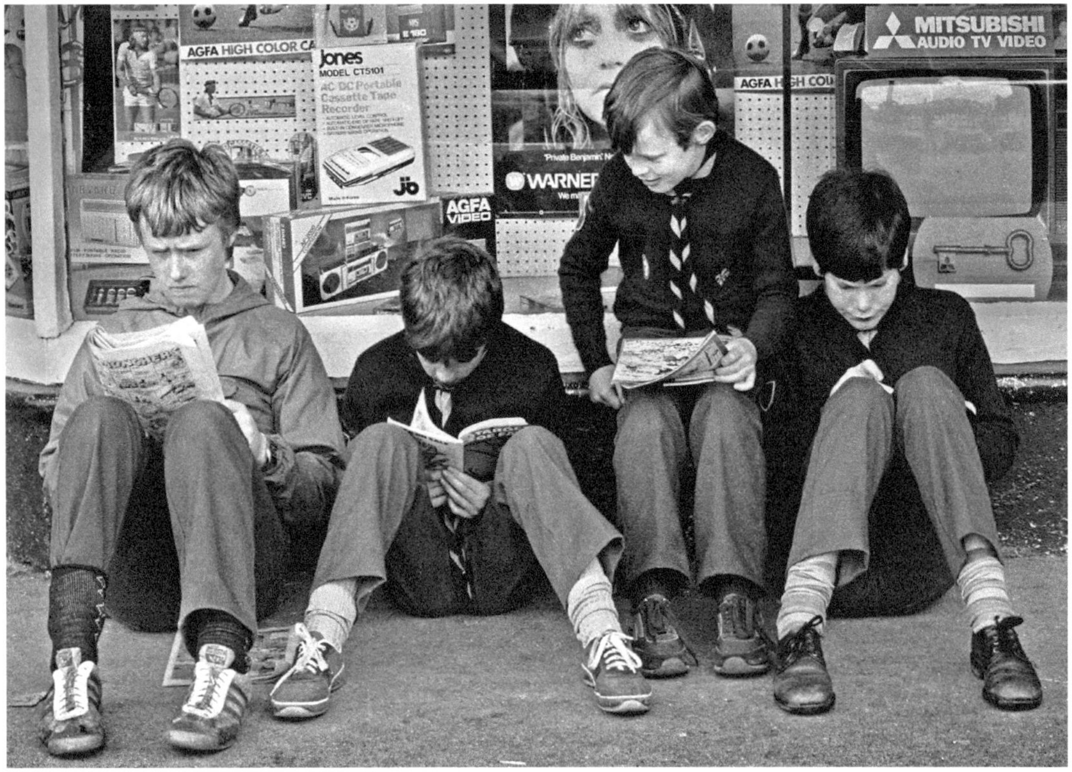

Reading the comics, near Charlestown, County Mayo, Ireland, 1984

The Natural Shoe Store, Dublin, County Dublin, Ireland, 1984

"I couldn't get an Irish manufacturer to make the kind of shoes I wanted, so I imported from Denmark, Holland, and Germany. I was selling shoes that were popular in Northern Europe—Birkenstock and Earth Shoes. The problem was that the main market for 'alternative' concepts were the young and educated—100,000 of whom left the country over the past few years because of the recession."

—Dermot O'Connor

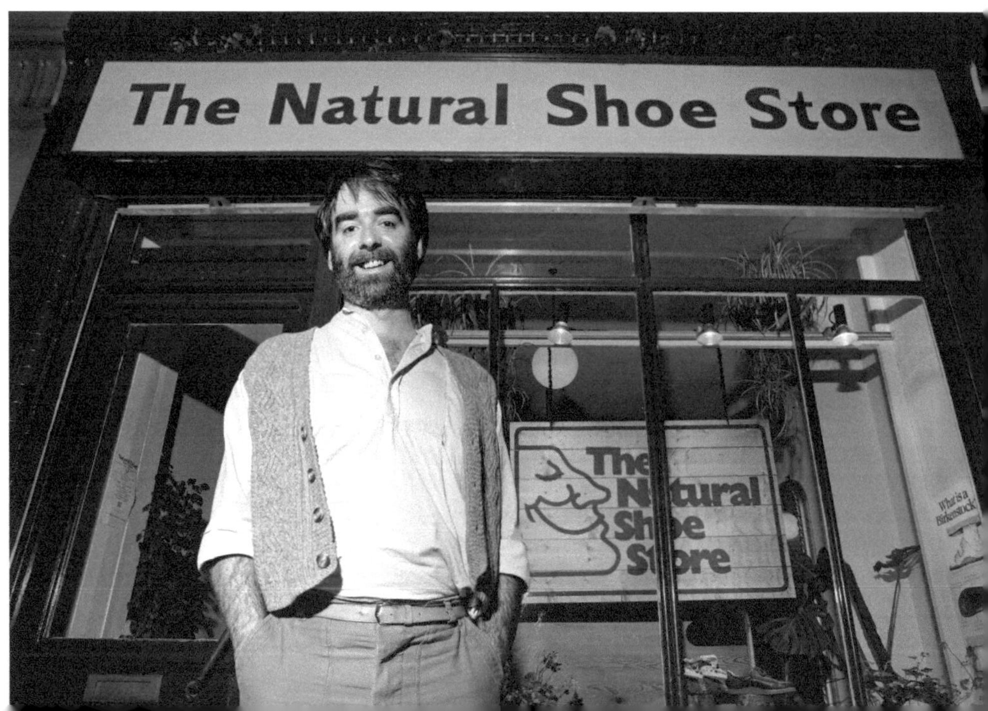

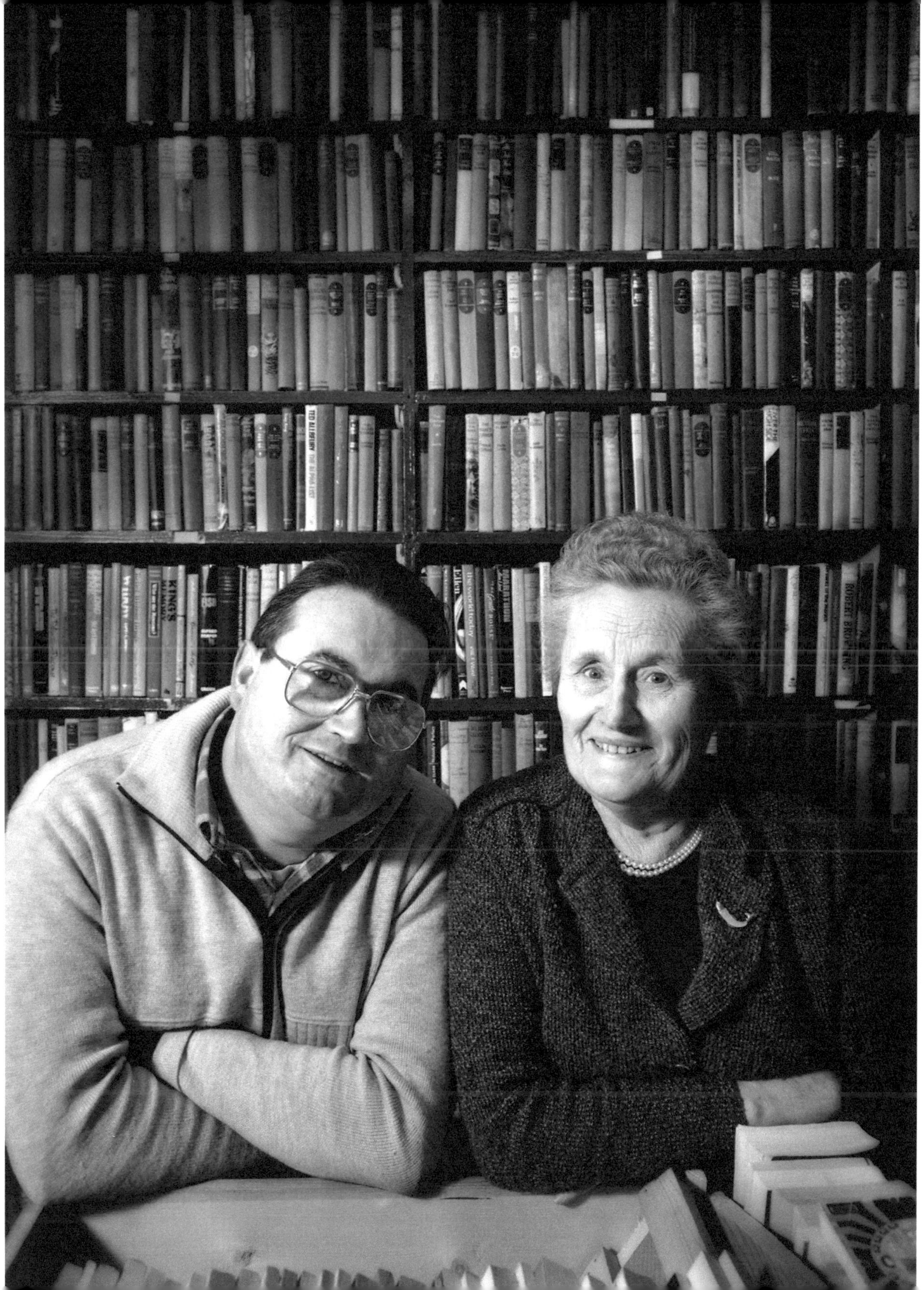

The Book Gallery, Ennis,
County Clare, Ireland, 1985

"I think I got my love of reading from my grandfather. No matter where I went on his farm, I'd find a book. I'd discover them in every room of the house, in the out-house, the hen-house, the reek of turf, niches in the walls, and even hidden away in rabbit burrows by the river."

—Seán Spellissy

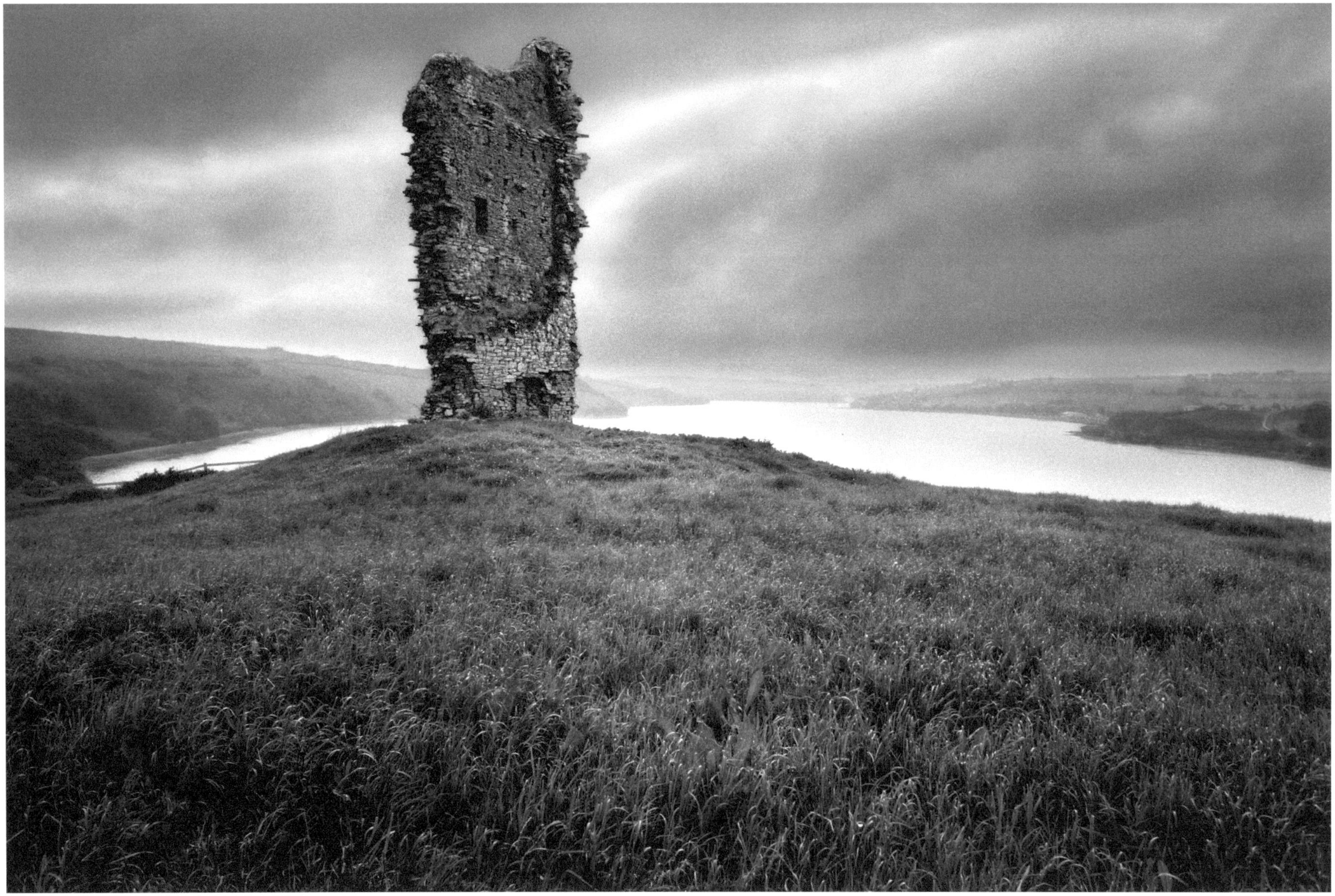

Ringrone Castle, Kinsale, County Cork, Ireland, 1982 *The lone sentinel still guarding the Bay of Kinsale, Ringrone Castle was built around 1223 and partially destroyed by the British in the 1601 siege of Kinsale. Fused with oxblood and stone, Ireland's castles could never be completely erased.*

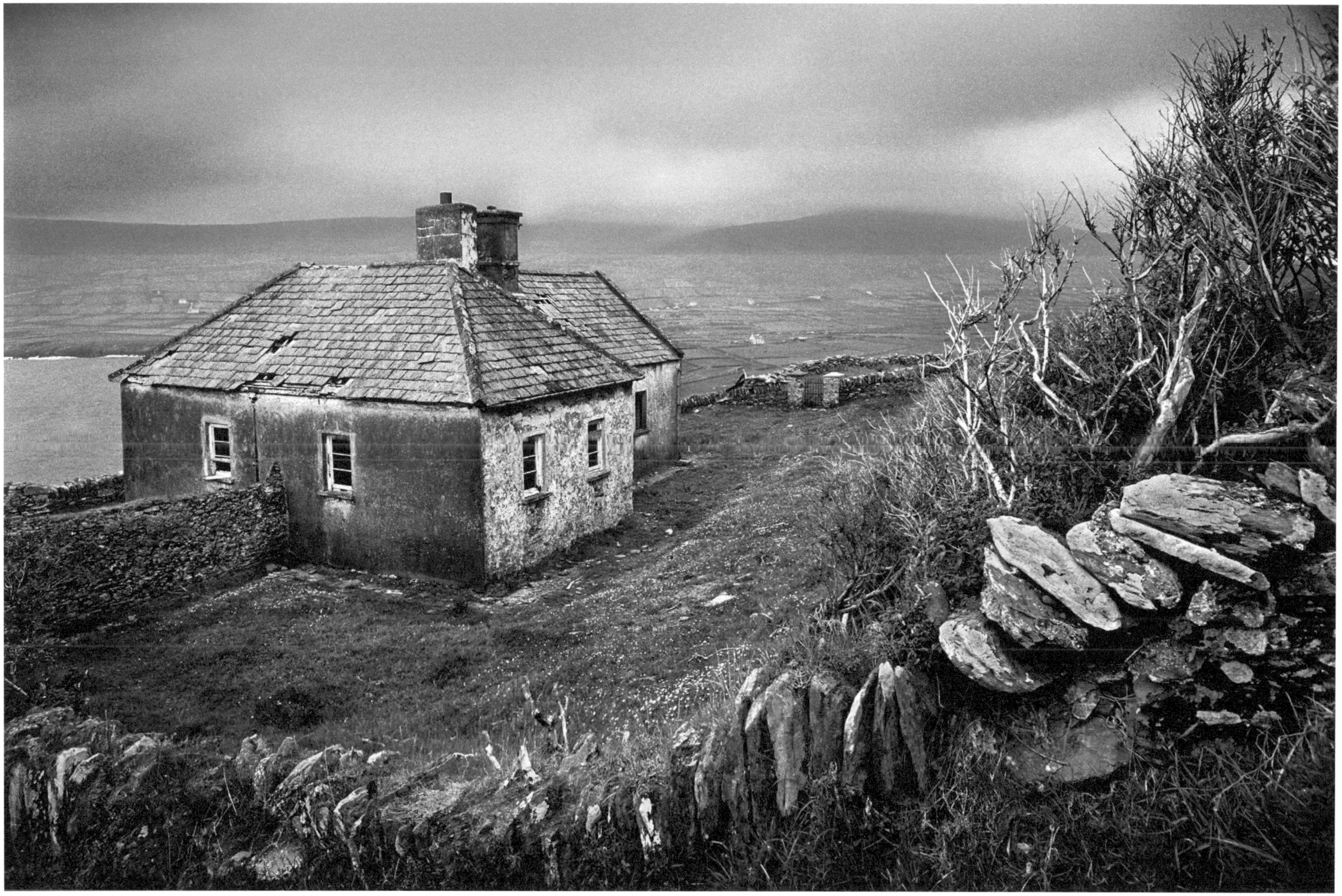

Former school house, North of Portmagee, County Kerry, Ireland, 1983 *"After he was lost at sea, the Banshee came. The latch of the gate was lifted but there was nobody there. And then there was this terrible keening that'll go through your heart, wailing up and down the yard." —Breda Barry*

THE NORTH
BEFORE GOOD FRIDAY

Downhill, Northern Ireland, 1982

Oh love, my love, had you brought
me in the boat
My spirit and my spells would have
saved you from harm
For my power was strong over wind
and wave.

—Fishermen's Folksong

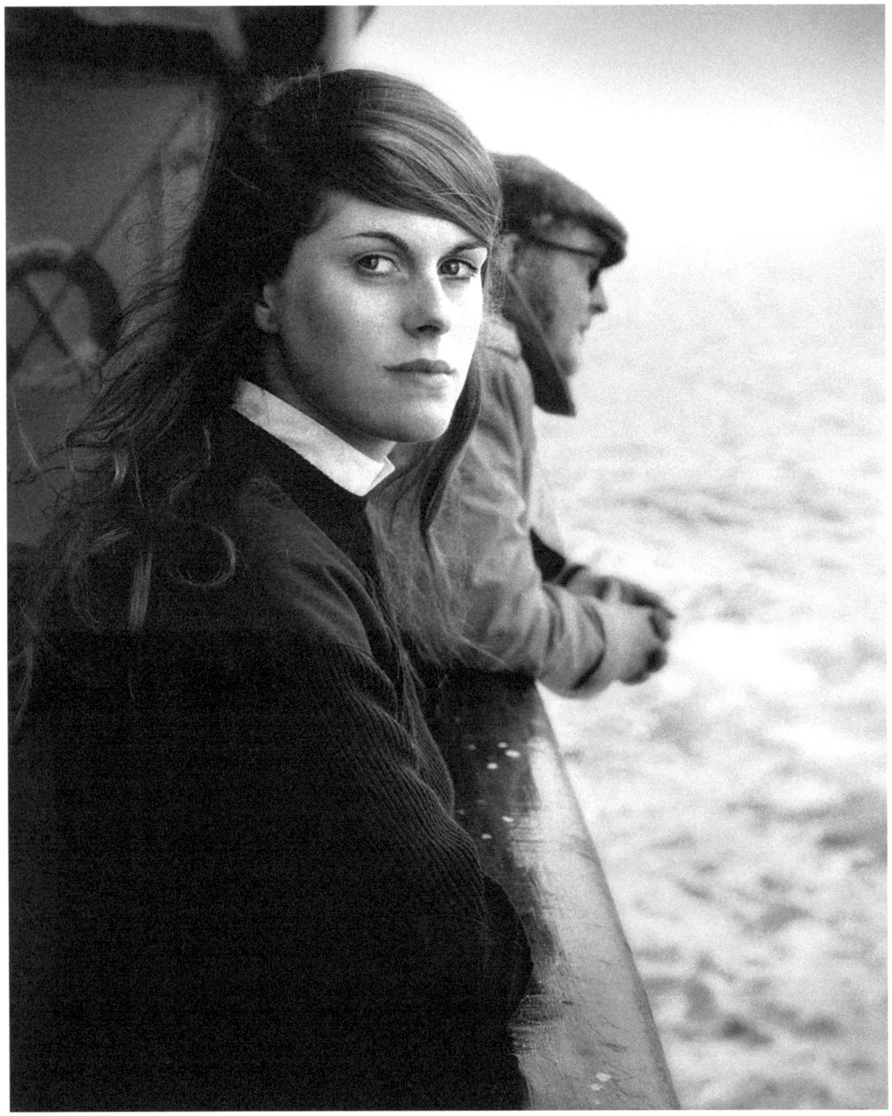

Cairnryan to Larne Ferry,
Northern Ireland, 1982

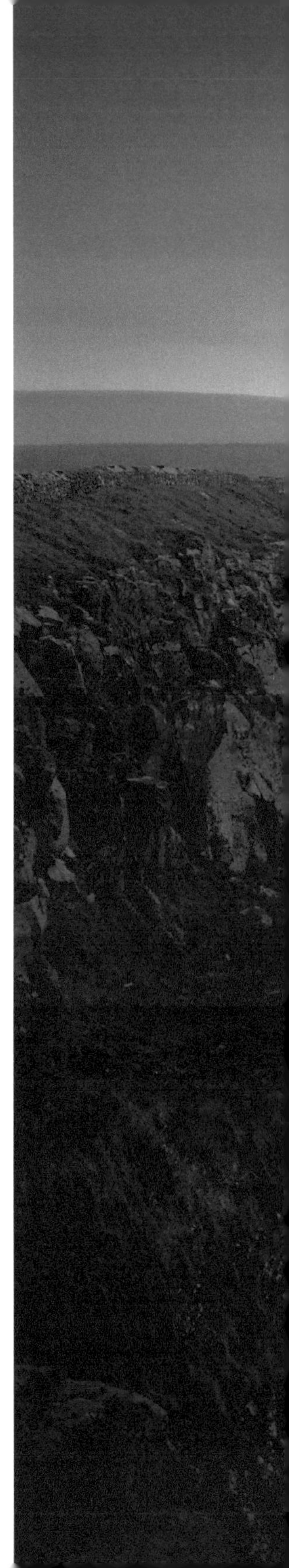

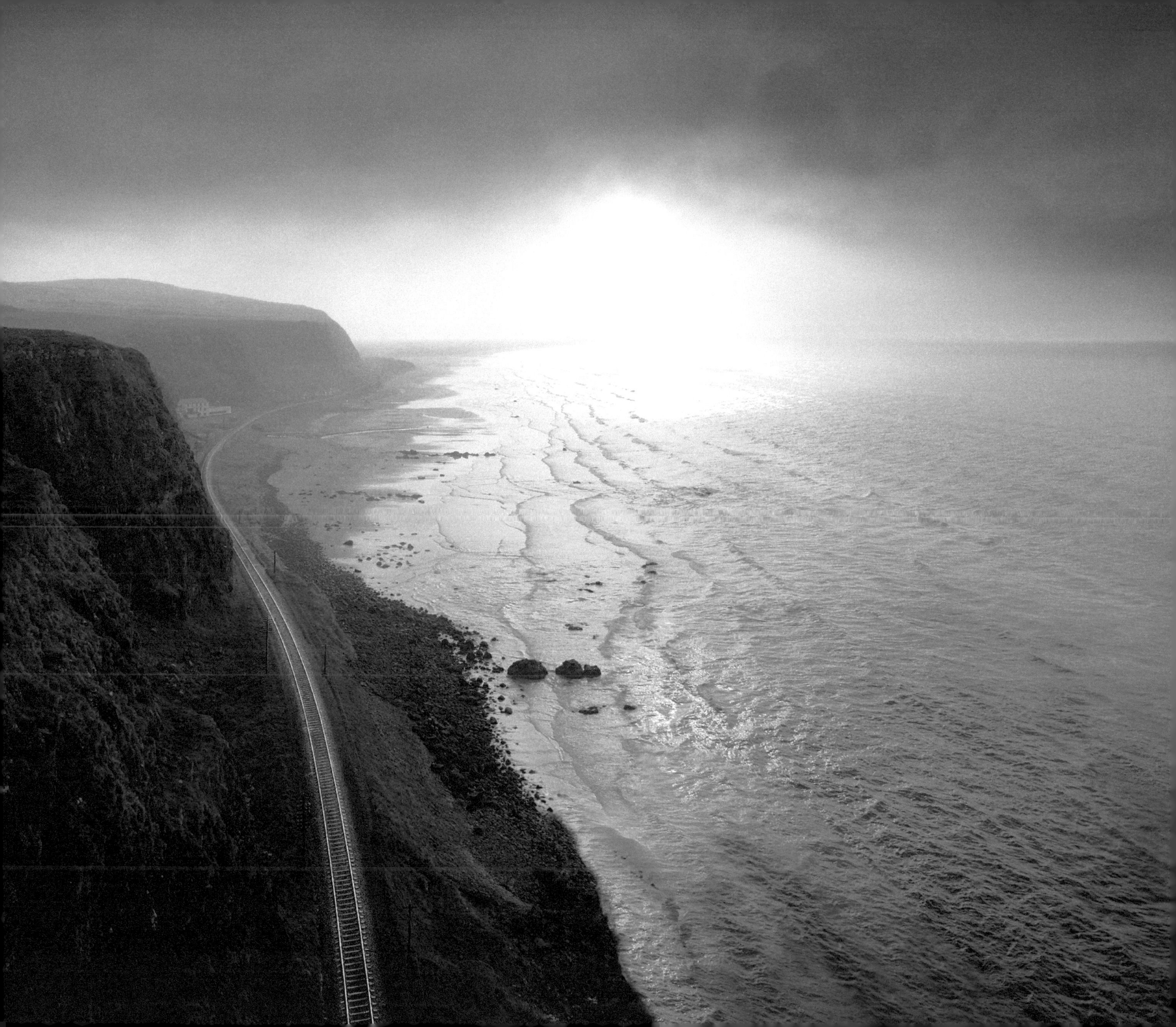

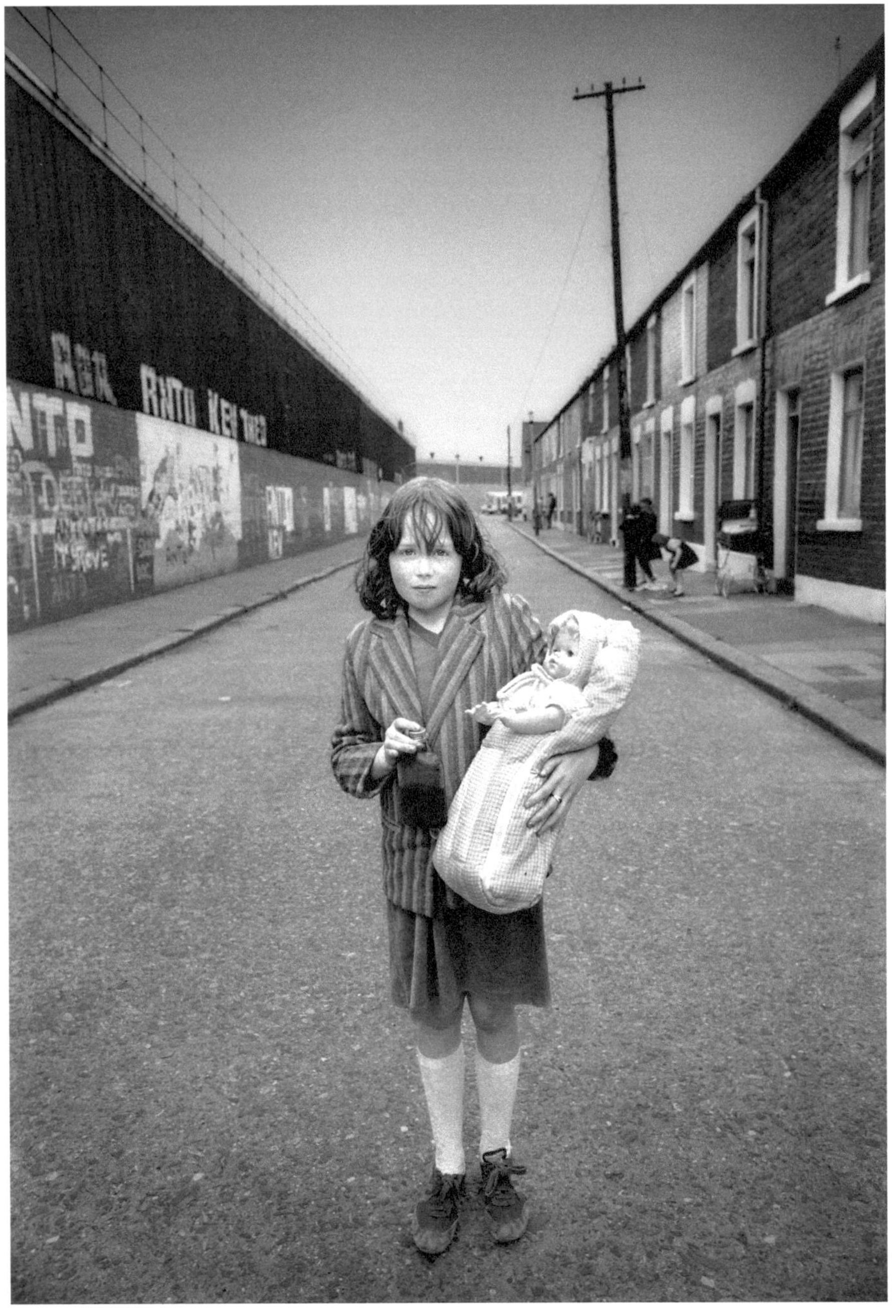

Control Zone, Belfast,
Northern Ireland, 1982

Street scene, Derry City,
Northern Ireland, 1982

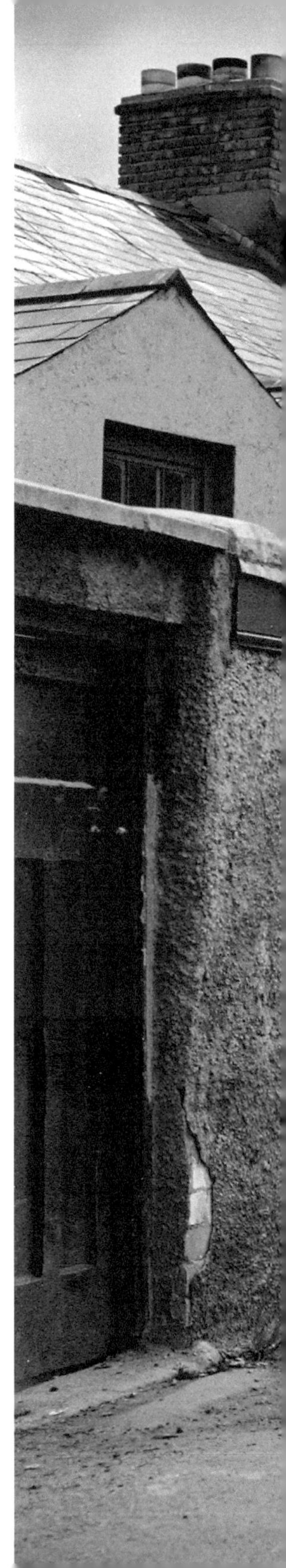

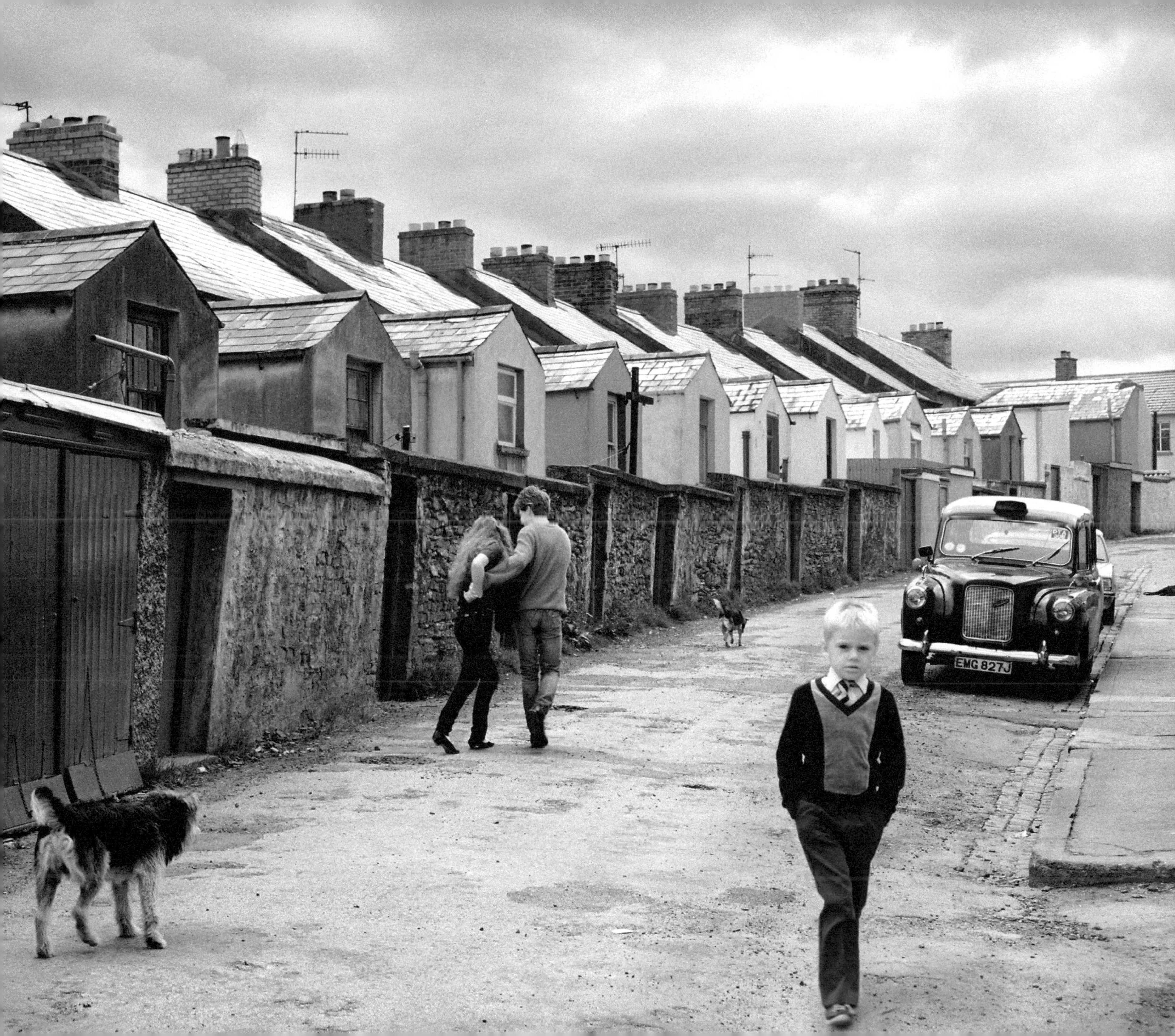
EMG 827J

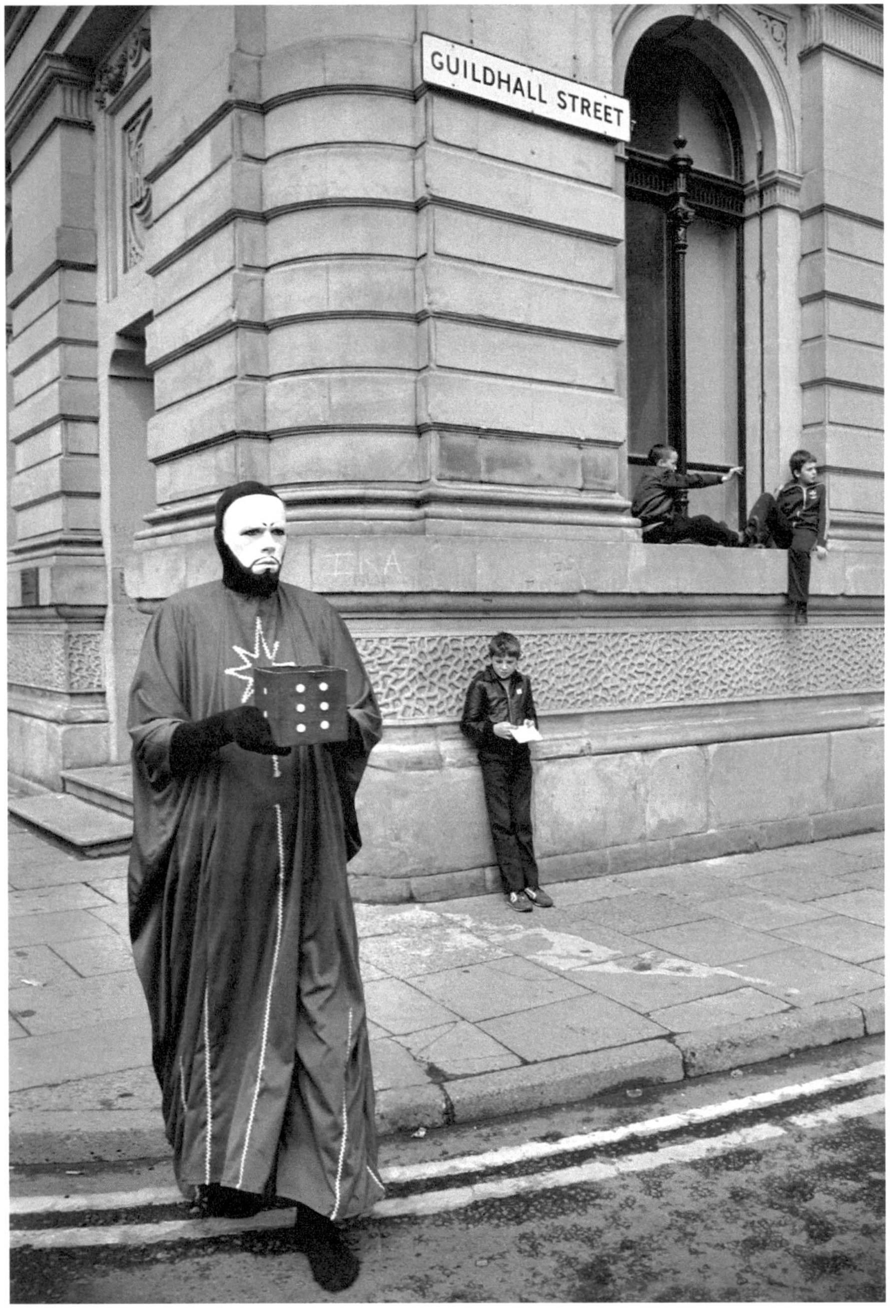

Courtney Brothers Traveling Circus,
Limevady, Northern Ireland, 1983

"I remember a hula hoop girl who performed through fire and smiled all the time in the ring. Out of the ring you could see her stomach covered in scars. And I remember riding the elephant and hanging on for dear life—the hair of the elephant is like wire and rubs uncomfortably against your thighs and yet I was waving and smiling. You are presenting joy and that contrast between pain and joy is part of the circus."

—Dea Birkett, The Irish Times, *July 28, 2018*

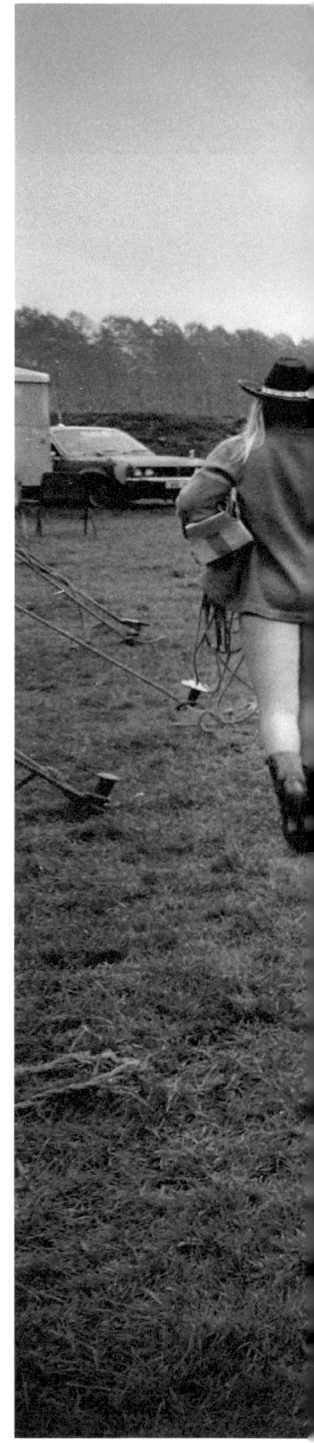

Mime, Derry City,
Northern Ireland, 1983

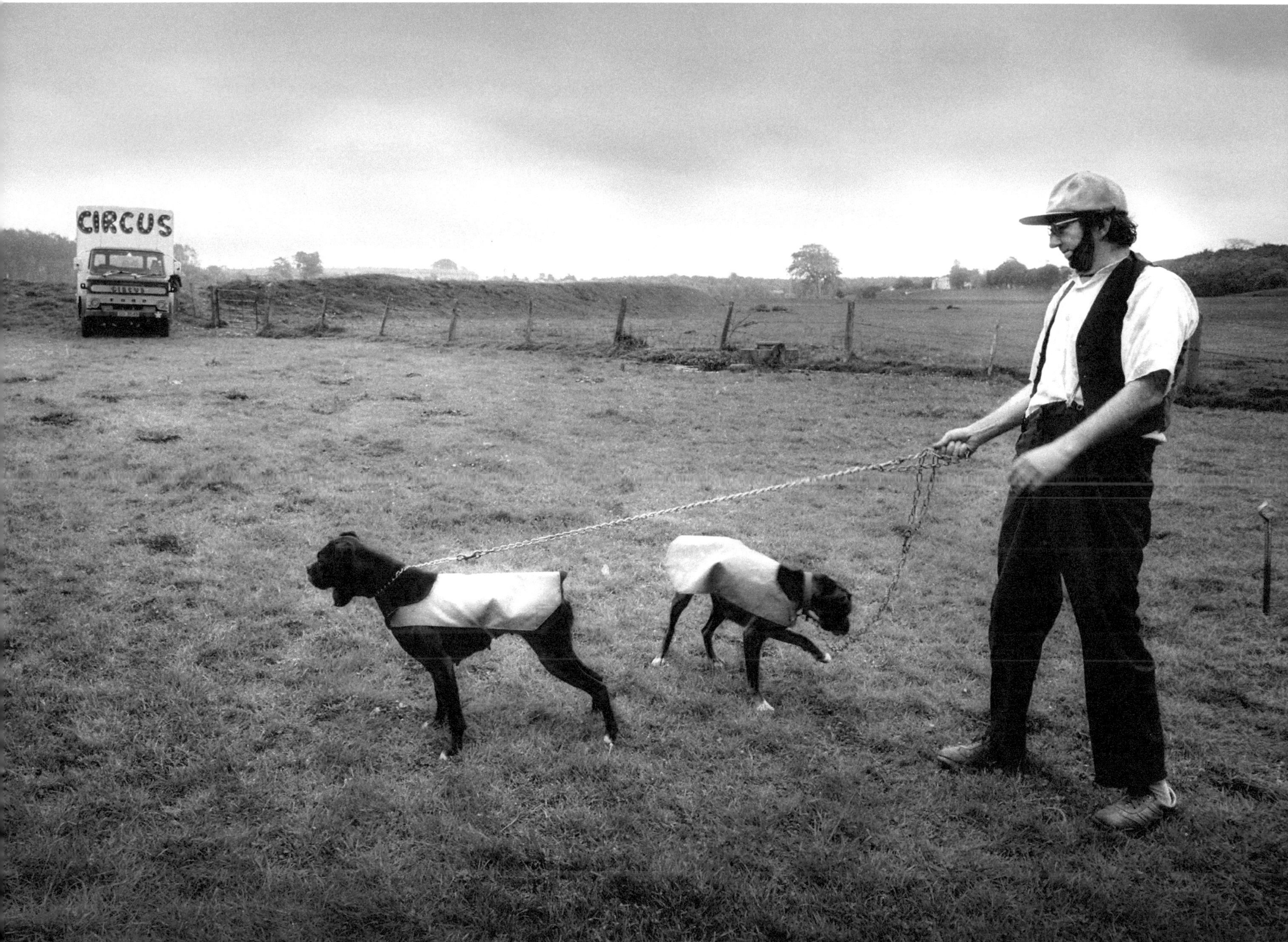
CIRCUS

Eglinton Stone Quarry,
Glenarm,
Northern Ireland, 1983

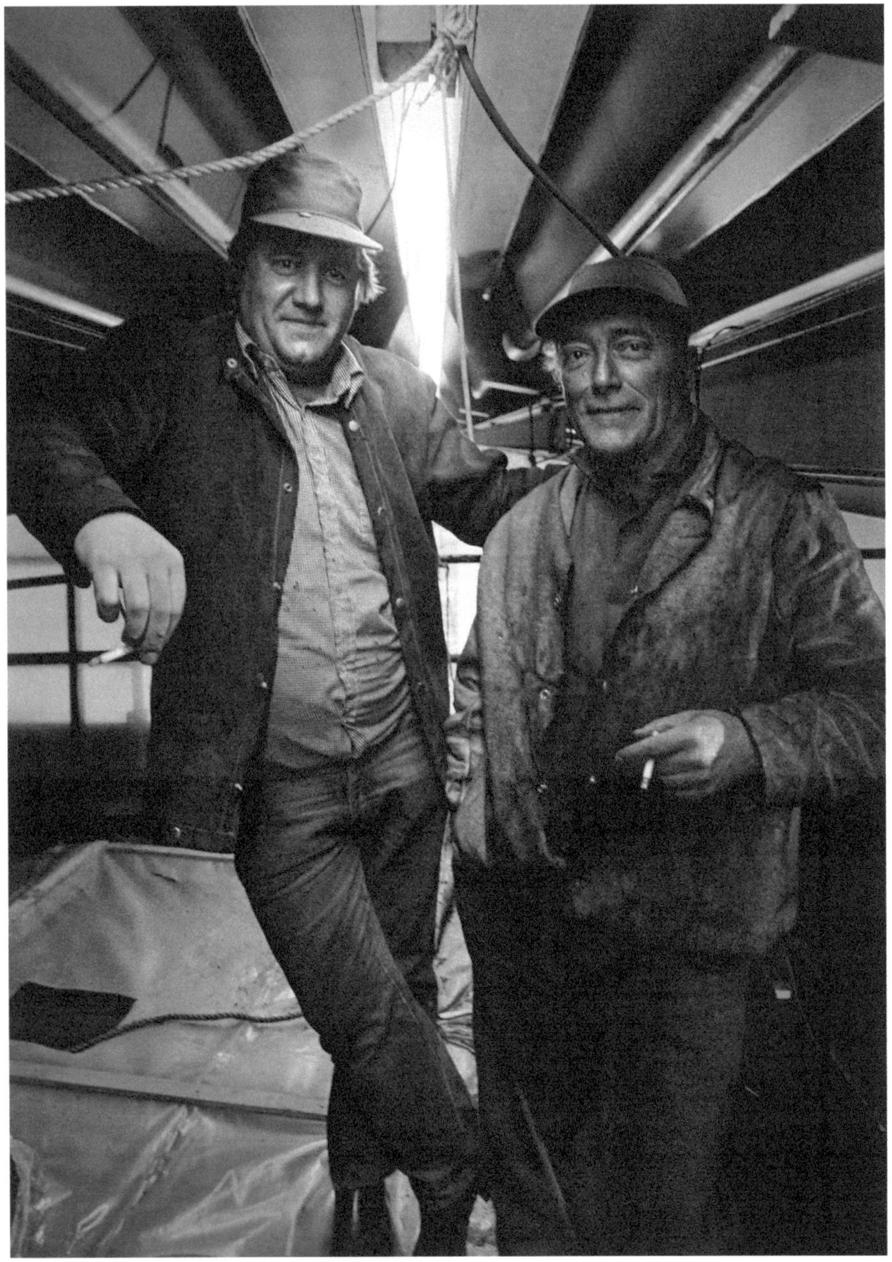

Bridge workers over the
River Foyle, Derry City,
Northern Ireland, 1982

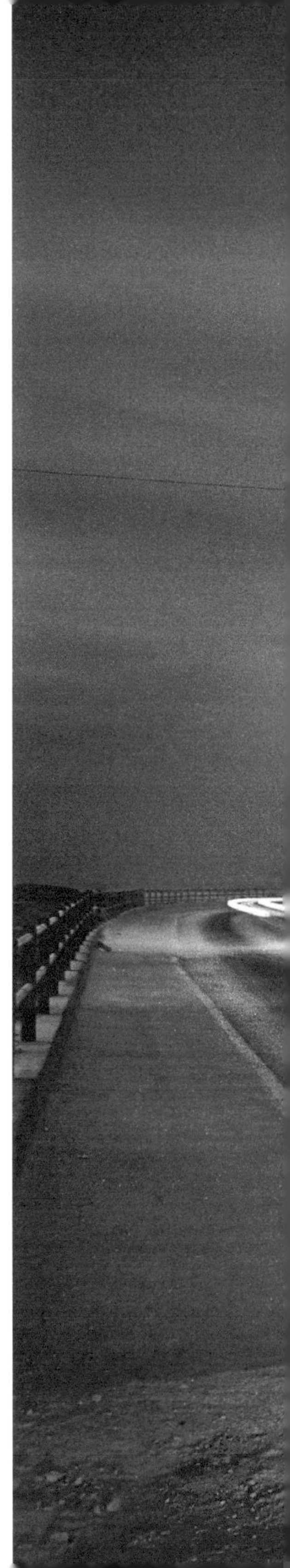

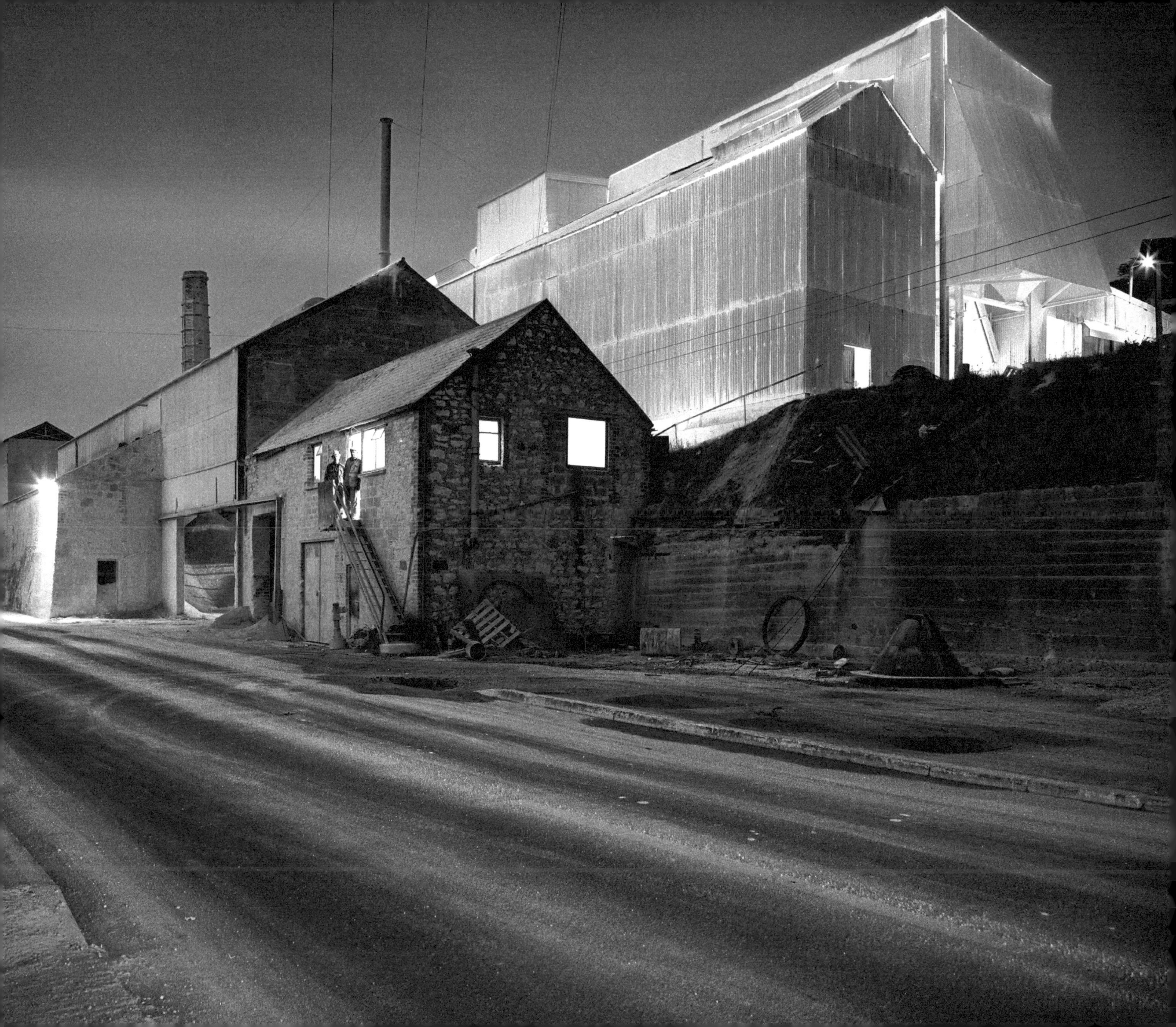

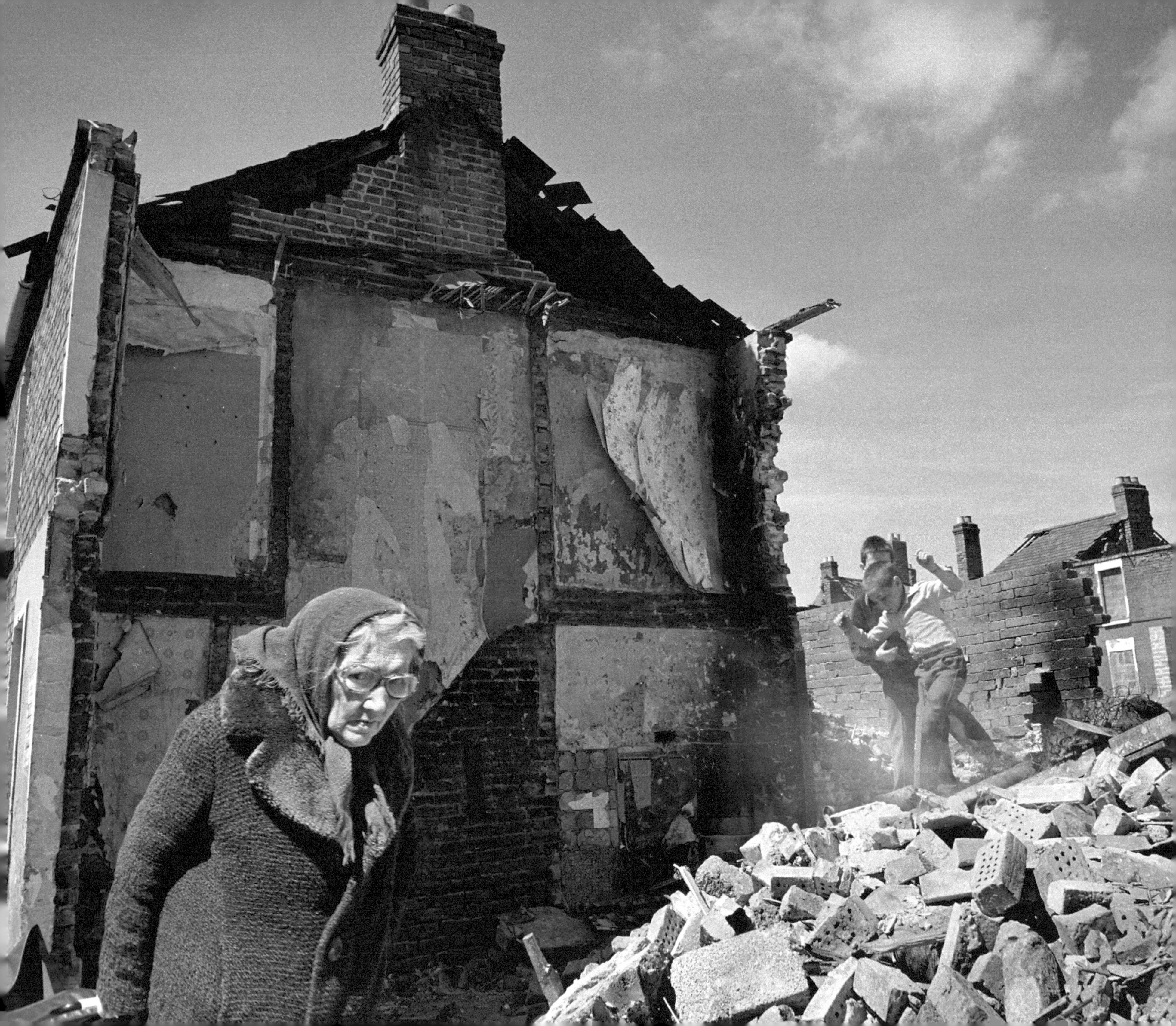

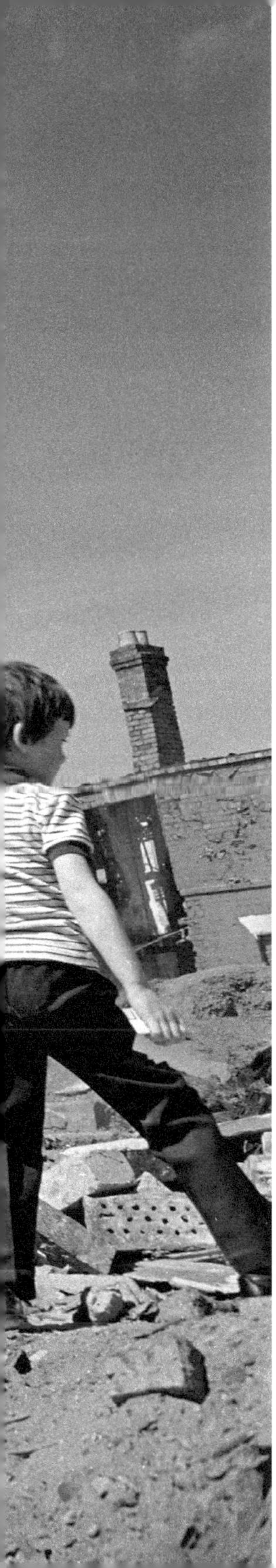

Falls Road neighborhood, West Belfast,
Northern Ireland, 1982

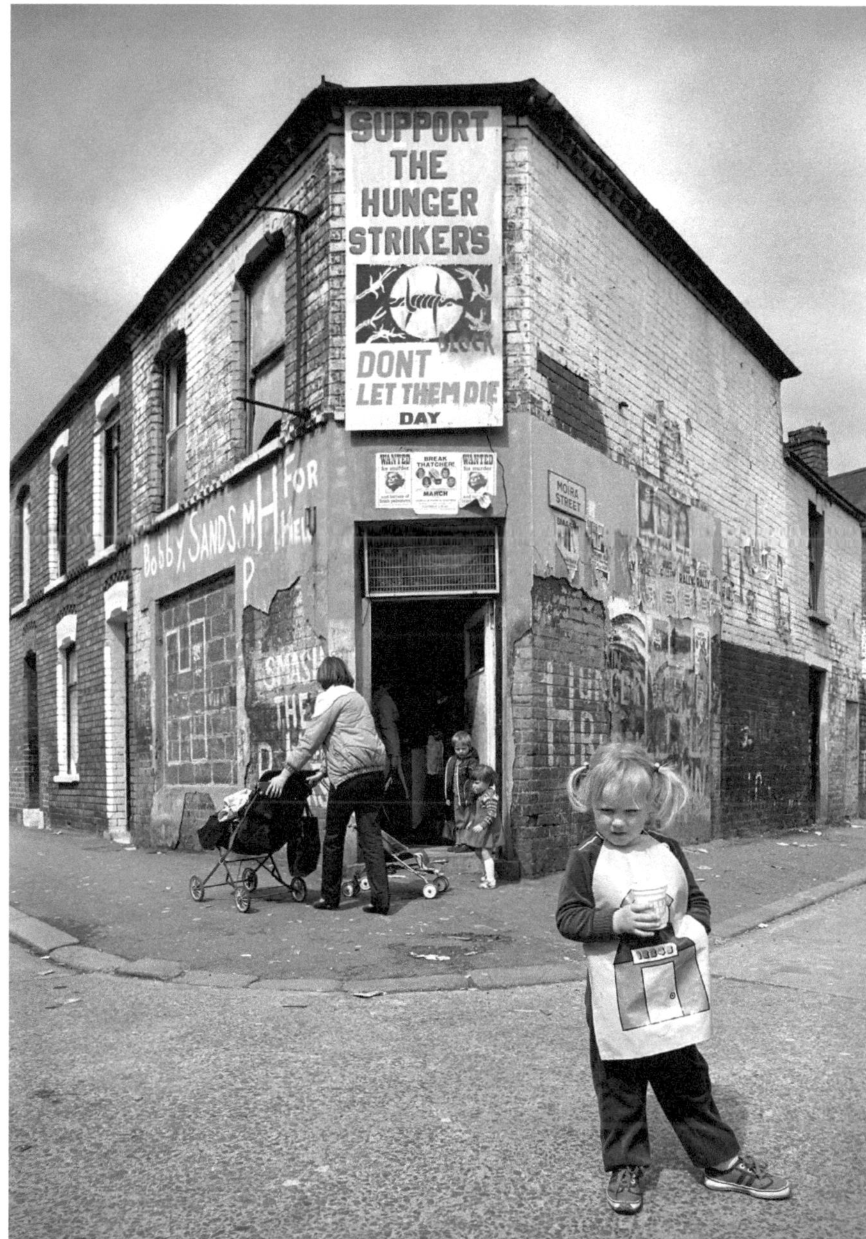

Hunger Strikers, Belfast,
Northern Ireland, 1982

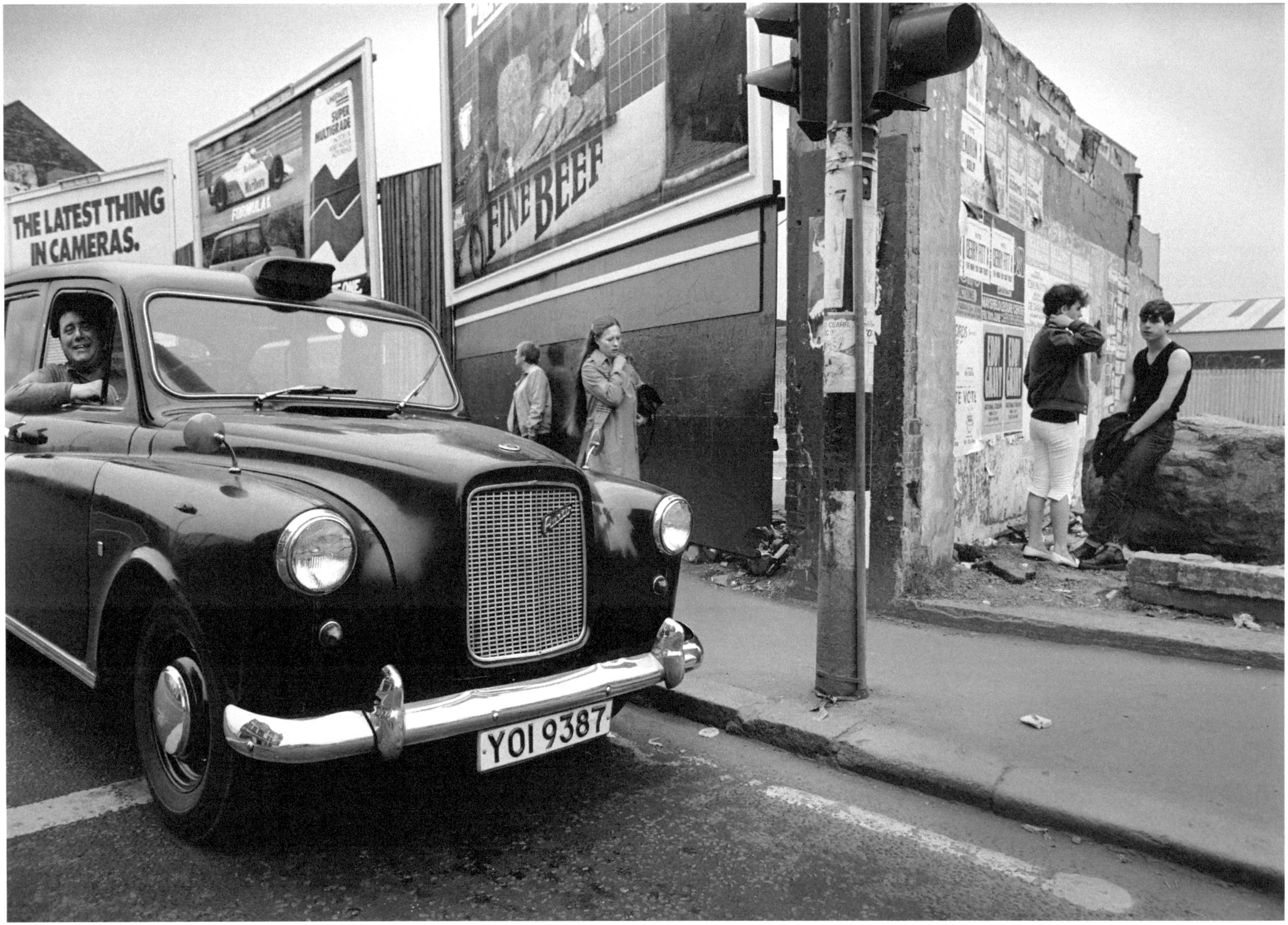

Black cab, Belfast, Northern Ireland, 1983

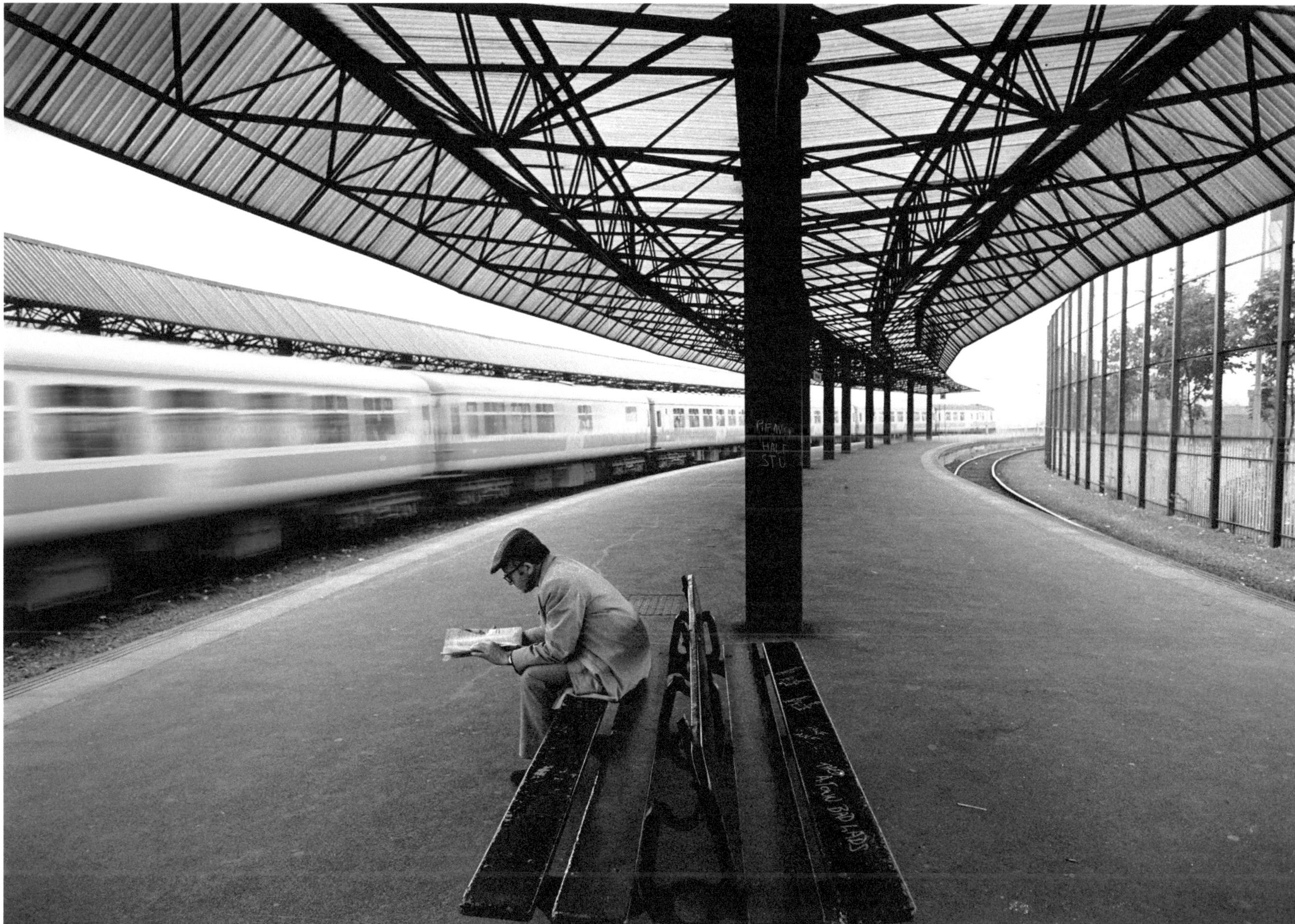

Central Train Station, Belfast, Northern Ireland, 1982

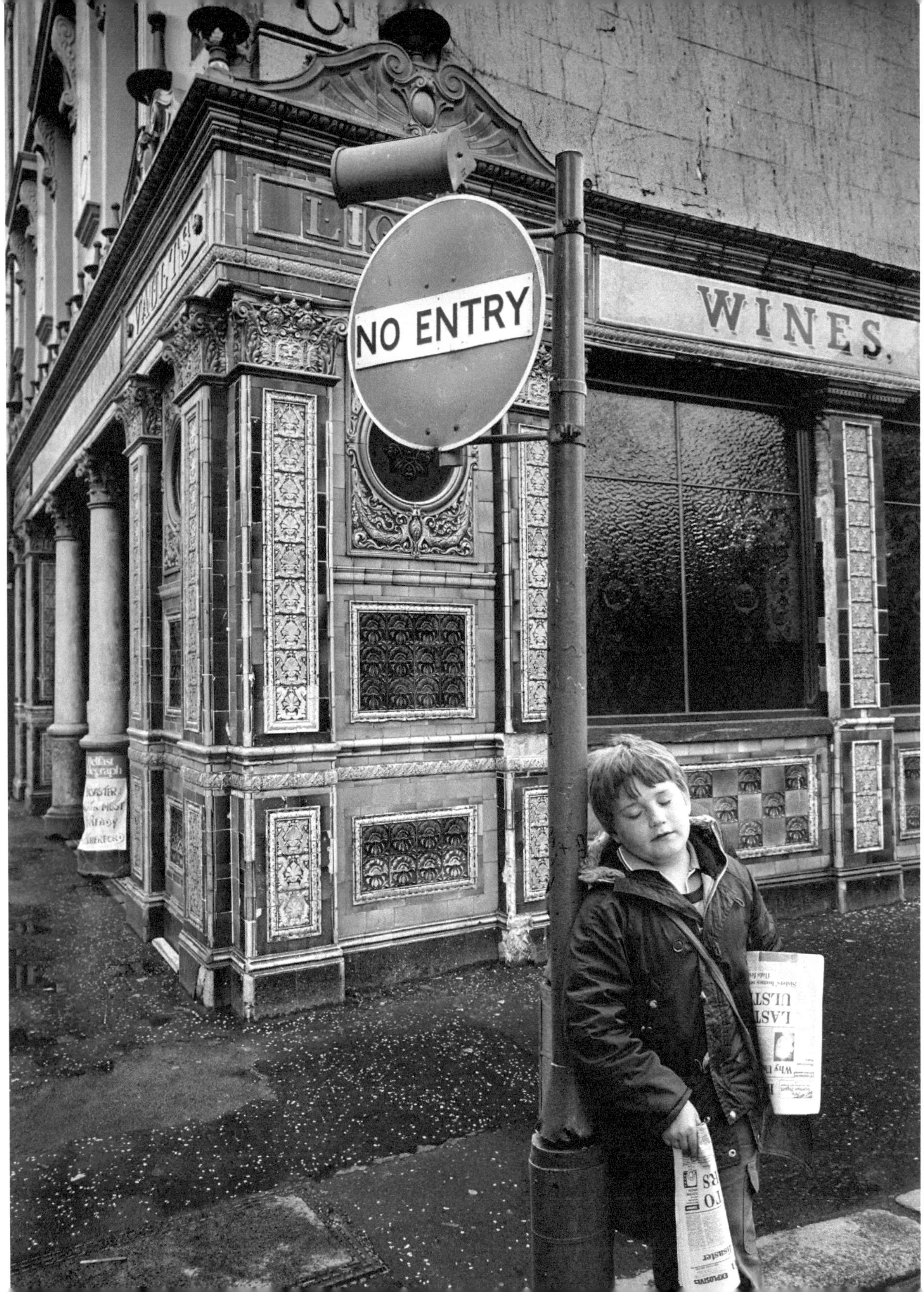

Newspaper boy, Belfast,
Northern Ireland, 1983

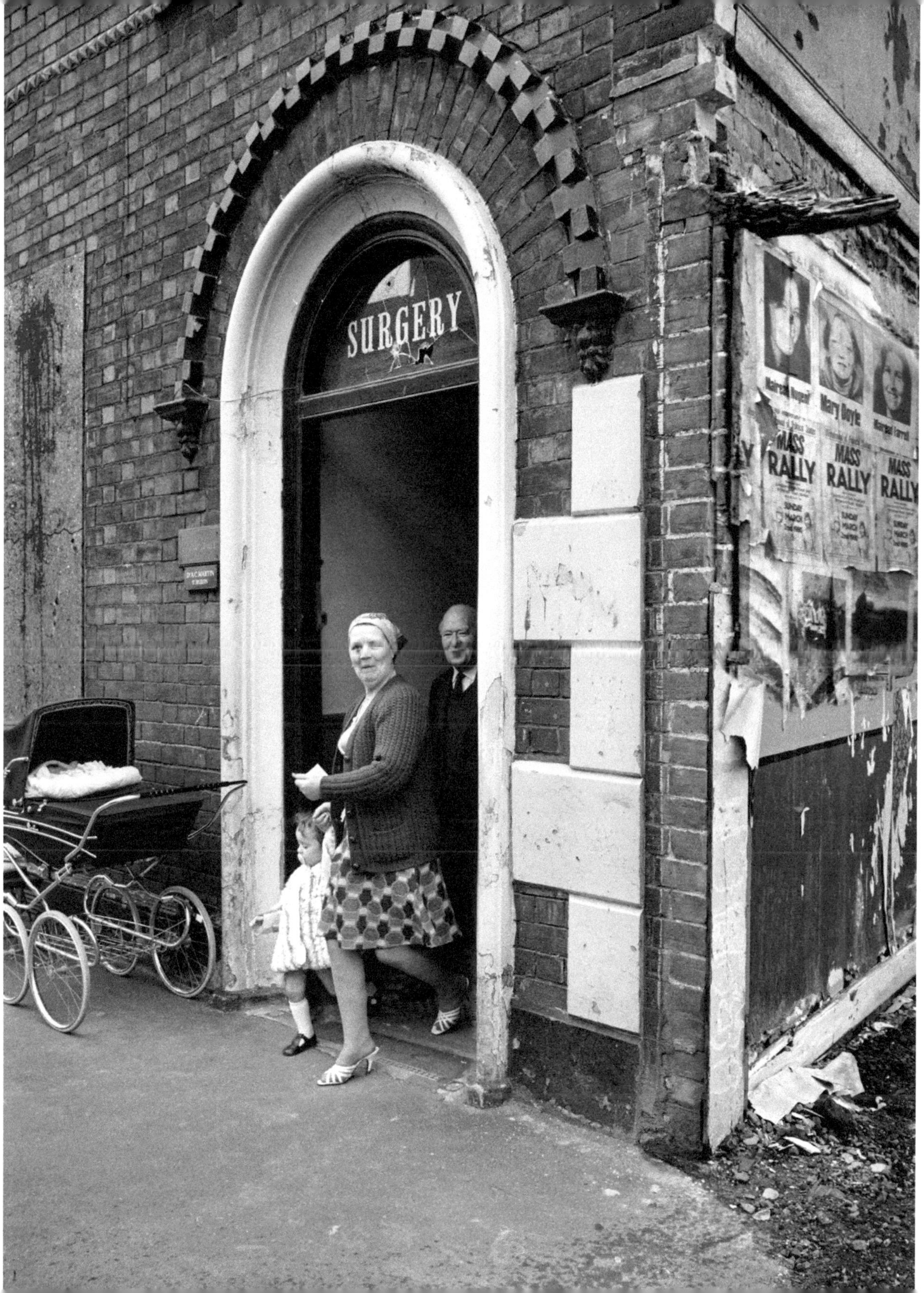

Surgery office, Belfast,
Northern Ireland, 1982

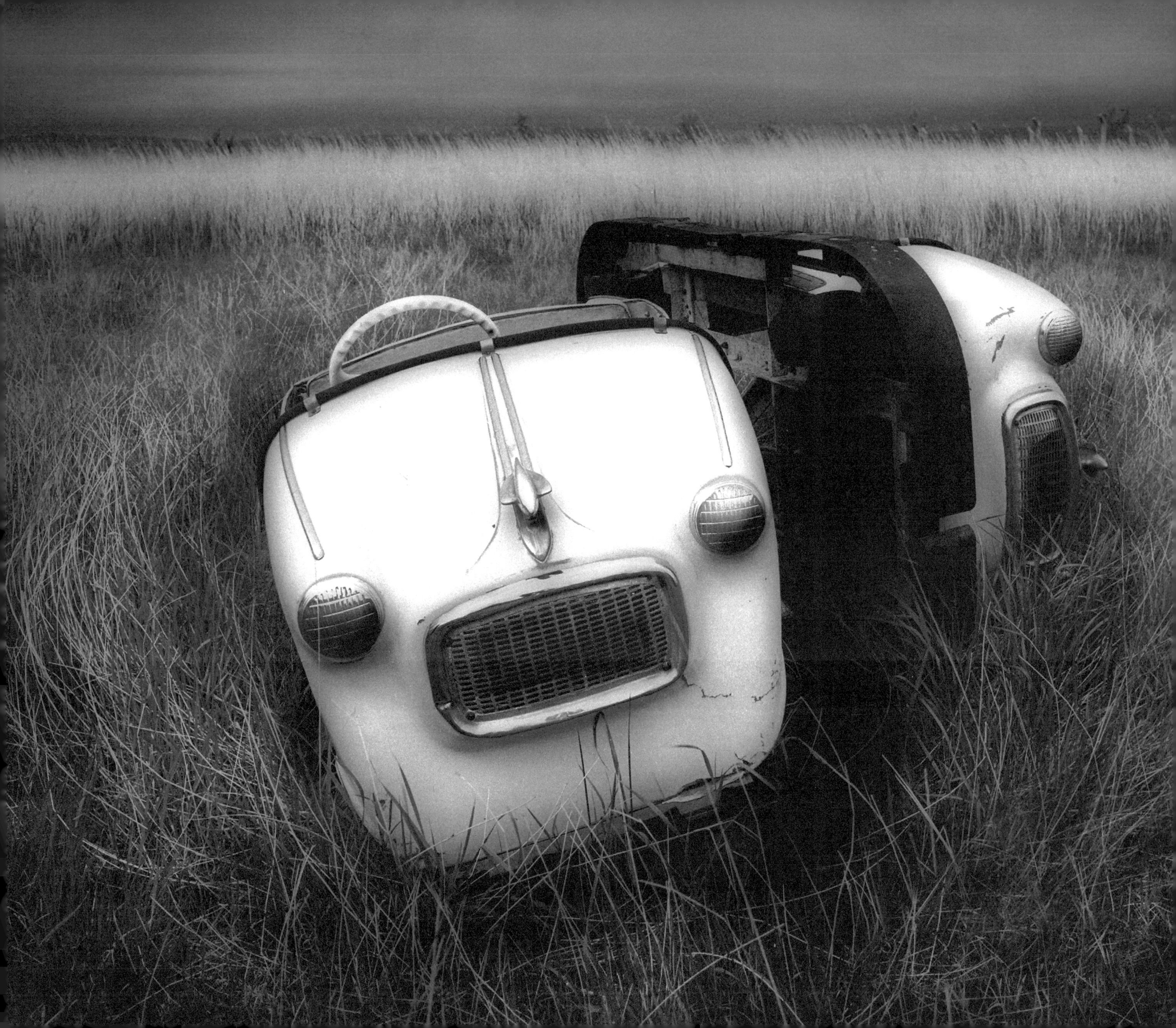

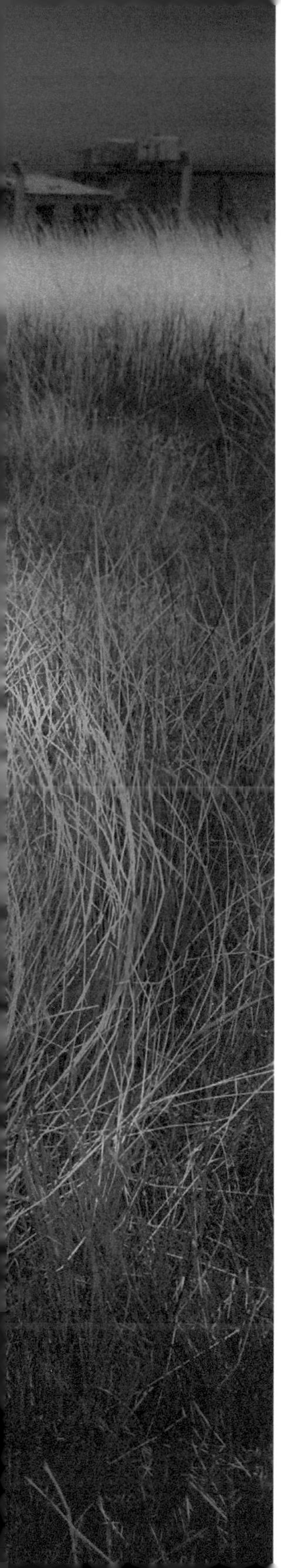

Dodgem cars in field,
near Portrush, Northern Ireland, 1982

"Barry's Amusement Park was the mecca of the young teenager first discovering girls, dodgems and fish and chips. Then joy of joys, at the age of 16 I was given a part time job for the summer holidays on the dodgem cars. I must have sent Barry's nearly broke with the free rides I gave to my friends. Ah, halcyon days!!"

—Michael White

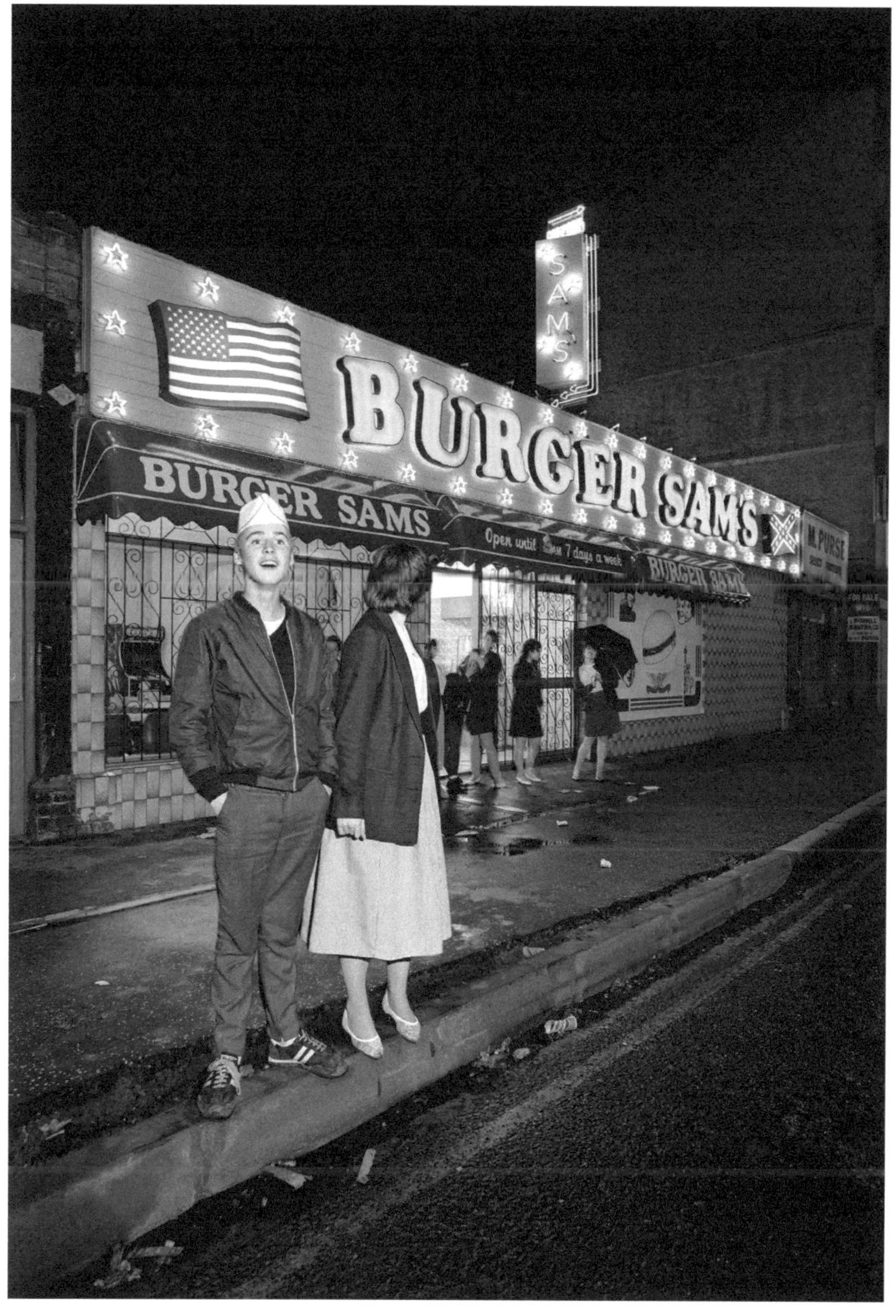

Burger Sam's, Belfast,
Northern Ireland, 1983

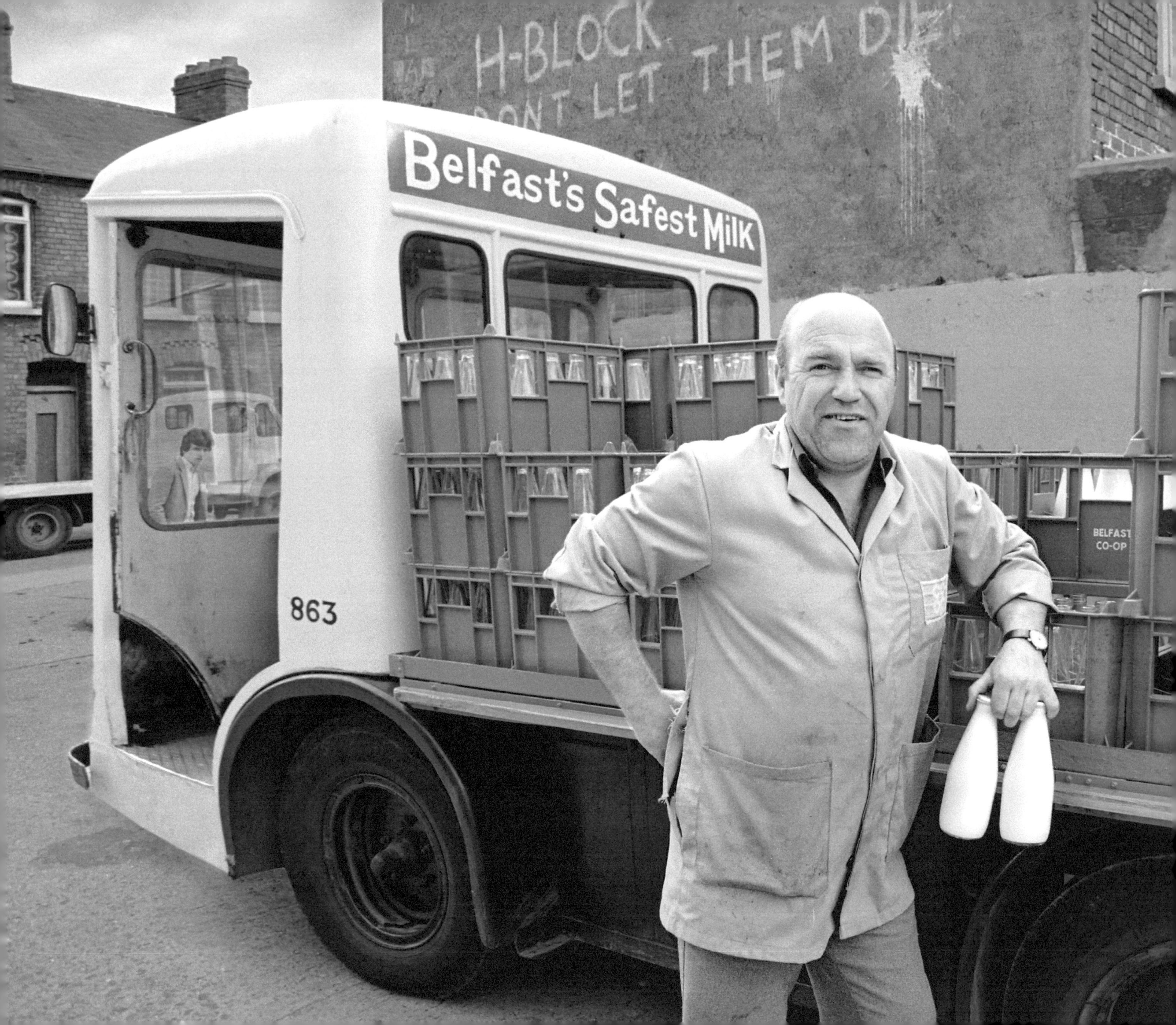
H-BLOCK
LET THEM
Belfast's Safest MilK
863
BELFAST
CO-OP

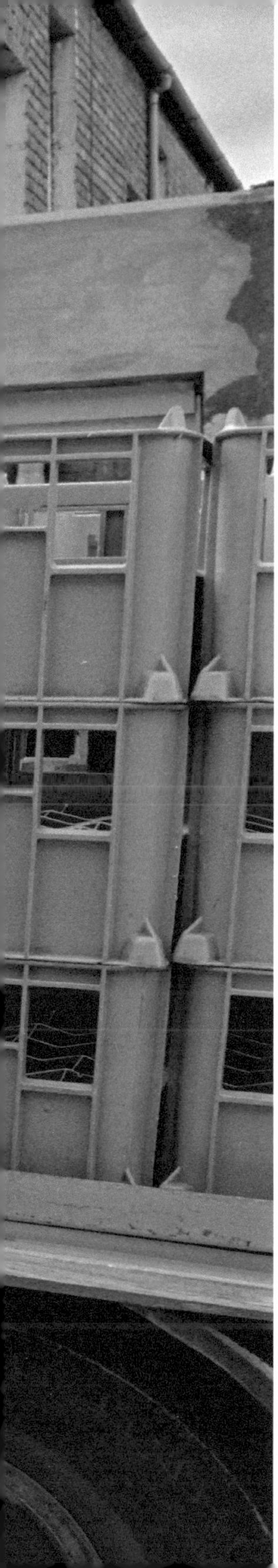

Milkman, Belfast,
Northern Ireland, 1982

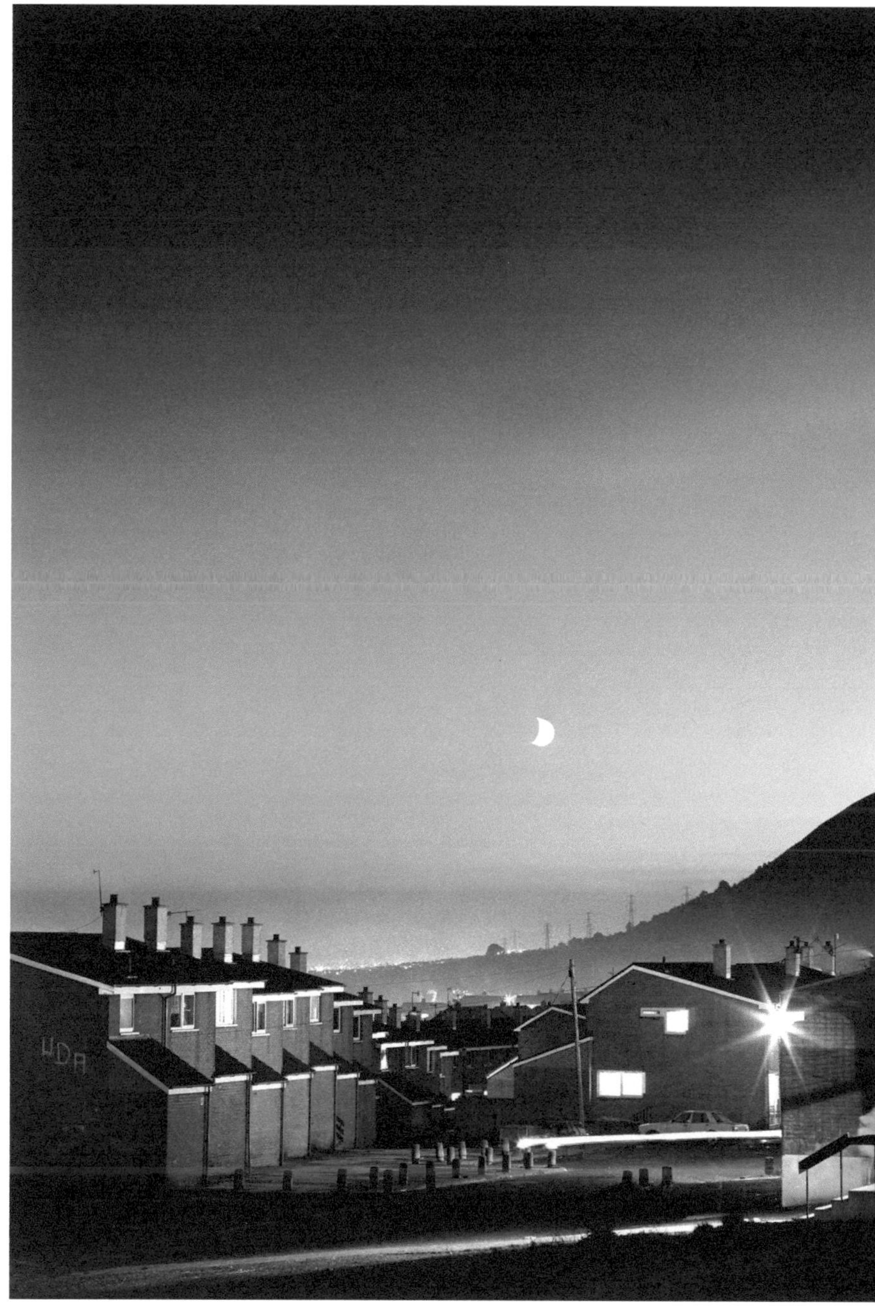

Protestant housing estate,
Belfast, Northern Ireland, 1982

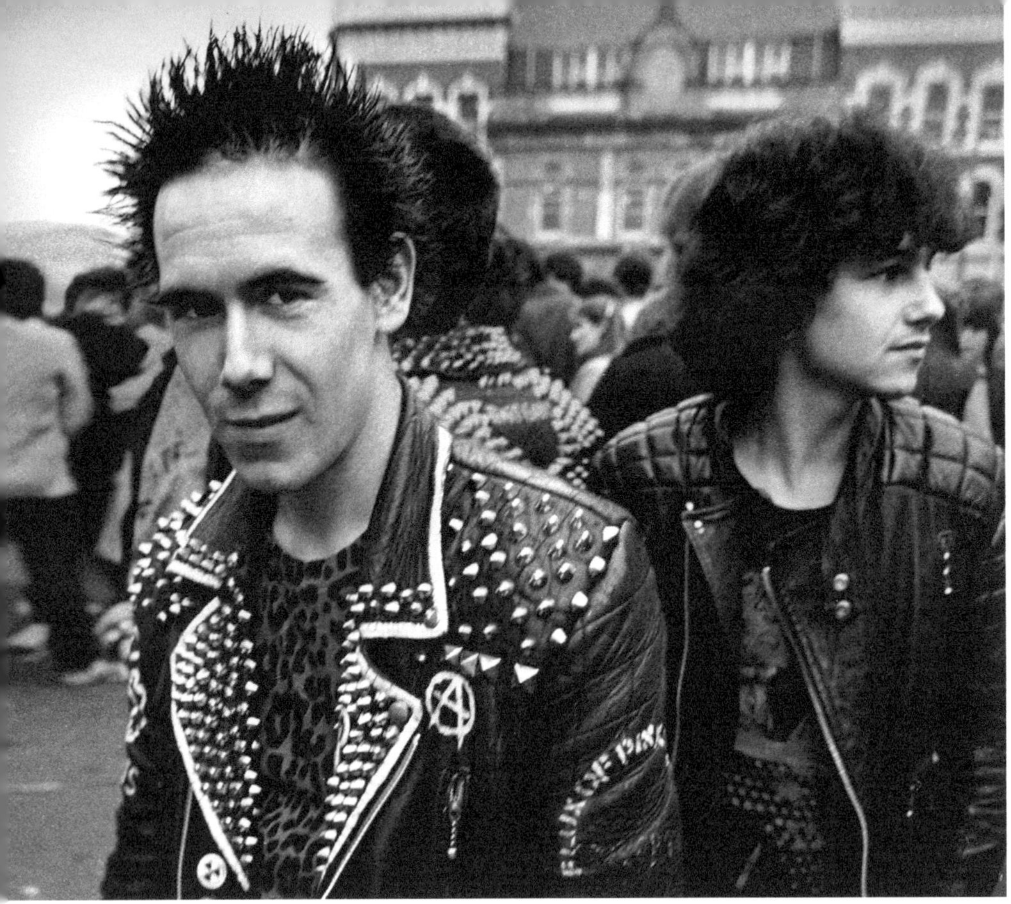

Derry City, Northern Ireland, 1982

"When I was about eleven, my mucker [buddy] Stevie McCartney told me about a punk band called the Sex Pistols who've a song out called 'God Save the Queen.' At that time it was the Queen's Jubilee. The British music chart was full of bands and songs paying homage to the Queen. We weren't big fans of the British establishment or the Queen, so I was surprised by Stevie's excited comments and dismissed them. Then Stevie told me that the song calls the Queen 'a fascist regime.' The record was banned in most parts of the UK and Northern Ireland, But Stevie—on a trip to Buncrana in the Irish Republic—got a copy. The minute I heard the song, I was knocked off my feet and was hooked."

—Malachy Daly

Pookiesnackenburger fiddler,
Derry City, Northern Ireland, 1983

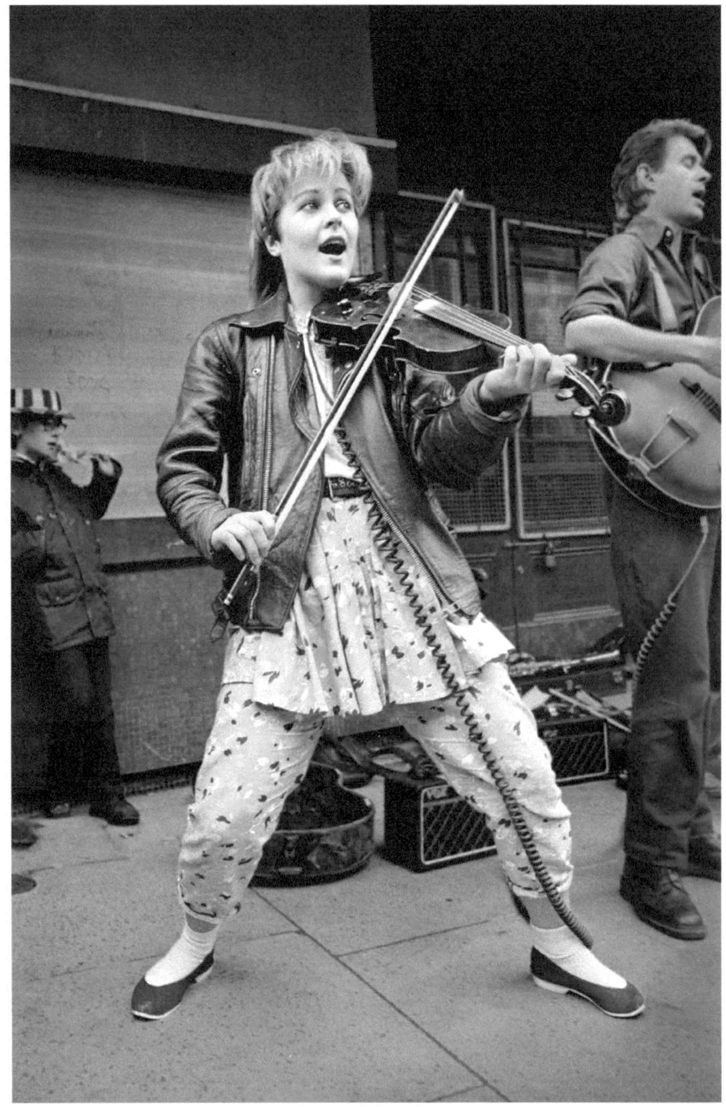

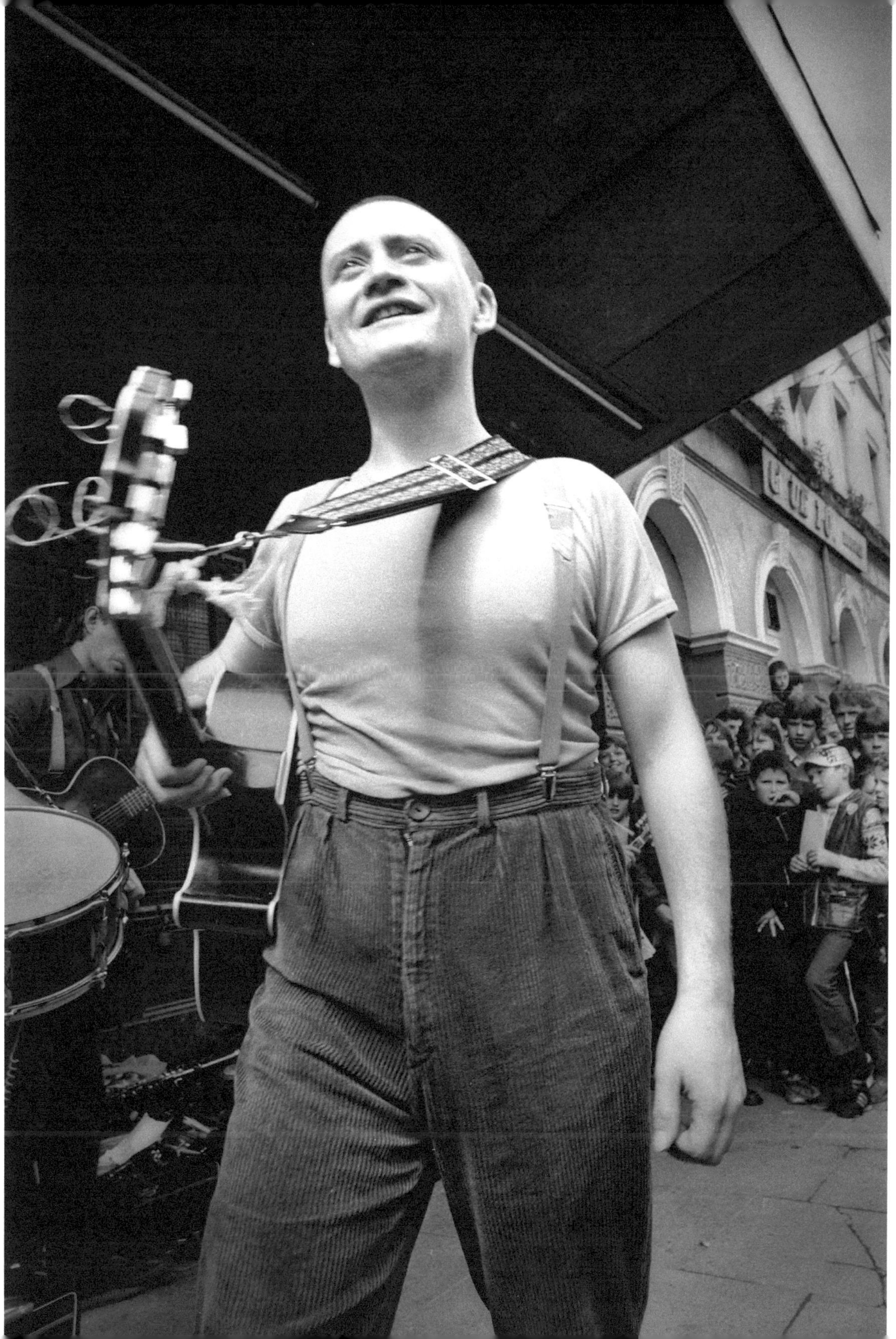

Pookiesnackenburger
street performer, Derry City,
Northern Ireland, 1983

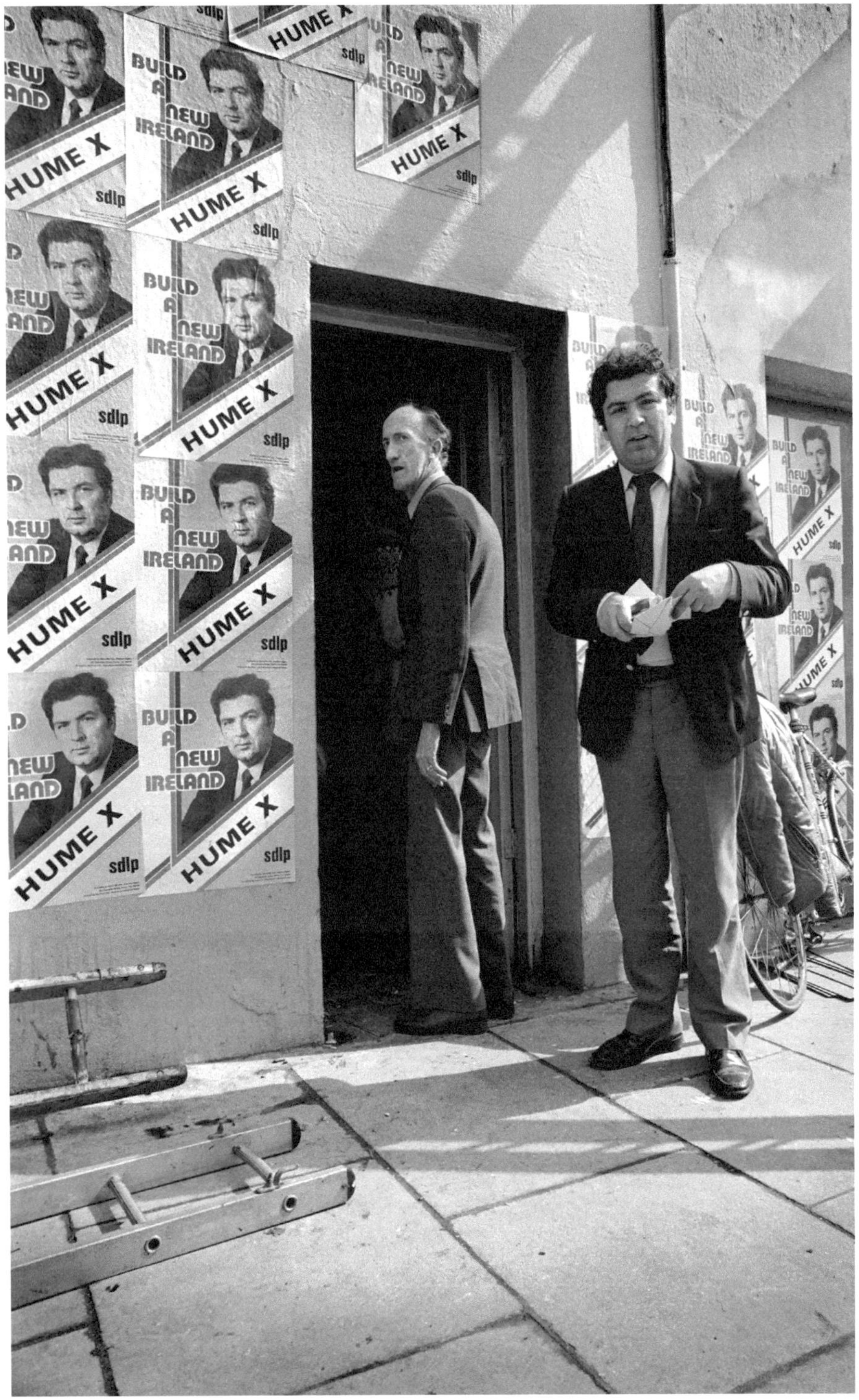

John Hume, founder of the Social Democratic Labor Party, outside SDLP headquarters, Derry City, Northern Ireland, 1982

The building's interior was burned the night before this photograph was taken. Ironically, there would be no lack of suspects given the SDLP's stated position of unifying Ireland through peaceful means and nonsectarian politics. But Hume would eventually prevail with the support of Sinn Fein leader Gerry Adams and Ulster Unionist Party leader David Trimble in bringing about the Good Friday Agreement of 1998 which established a power-sharing government for Northern Ireland. For this work, Hume and Trimble were awarded the Nobel Prize for Peace.

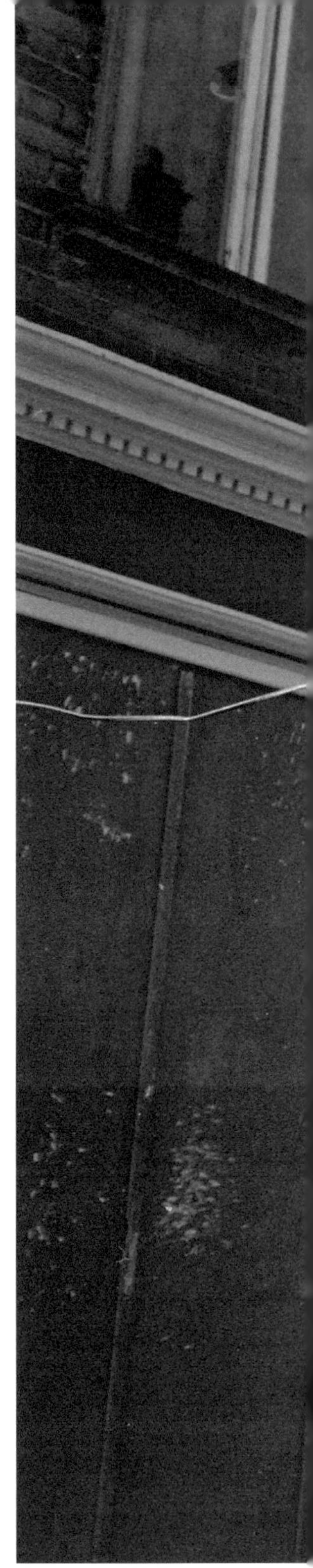

Control Zone border station,
South of Newry,
Northern Ireland, 1982

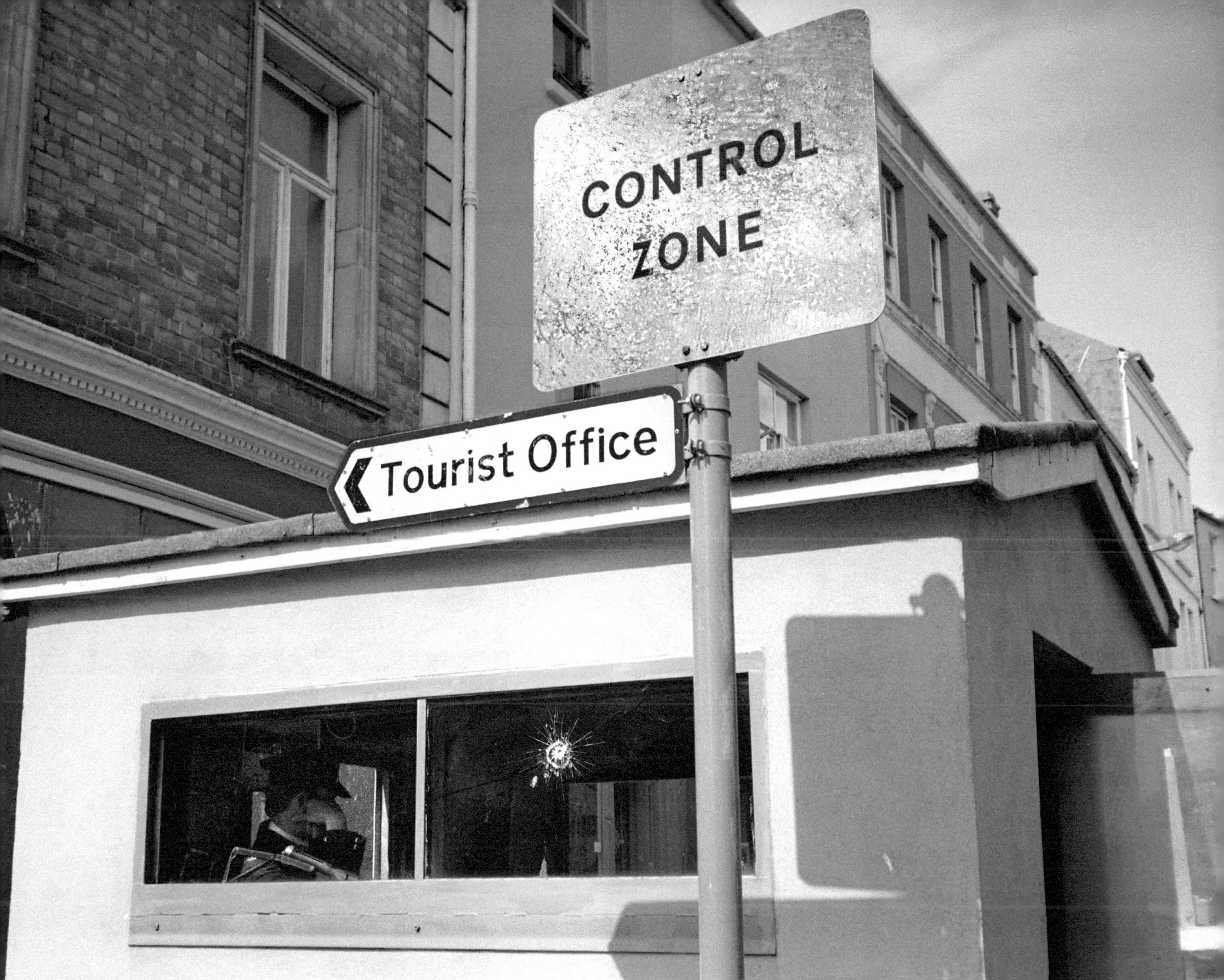
CONTROL
ZONE
Tourist Office

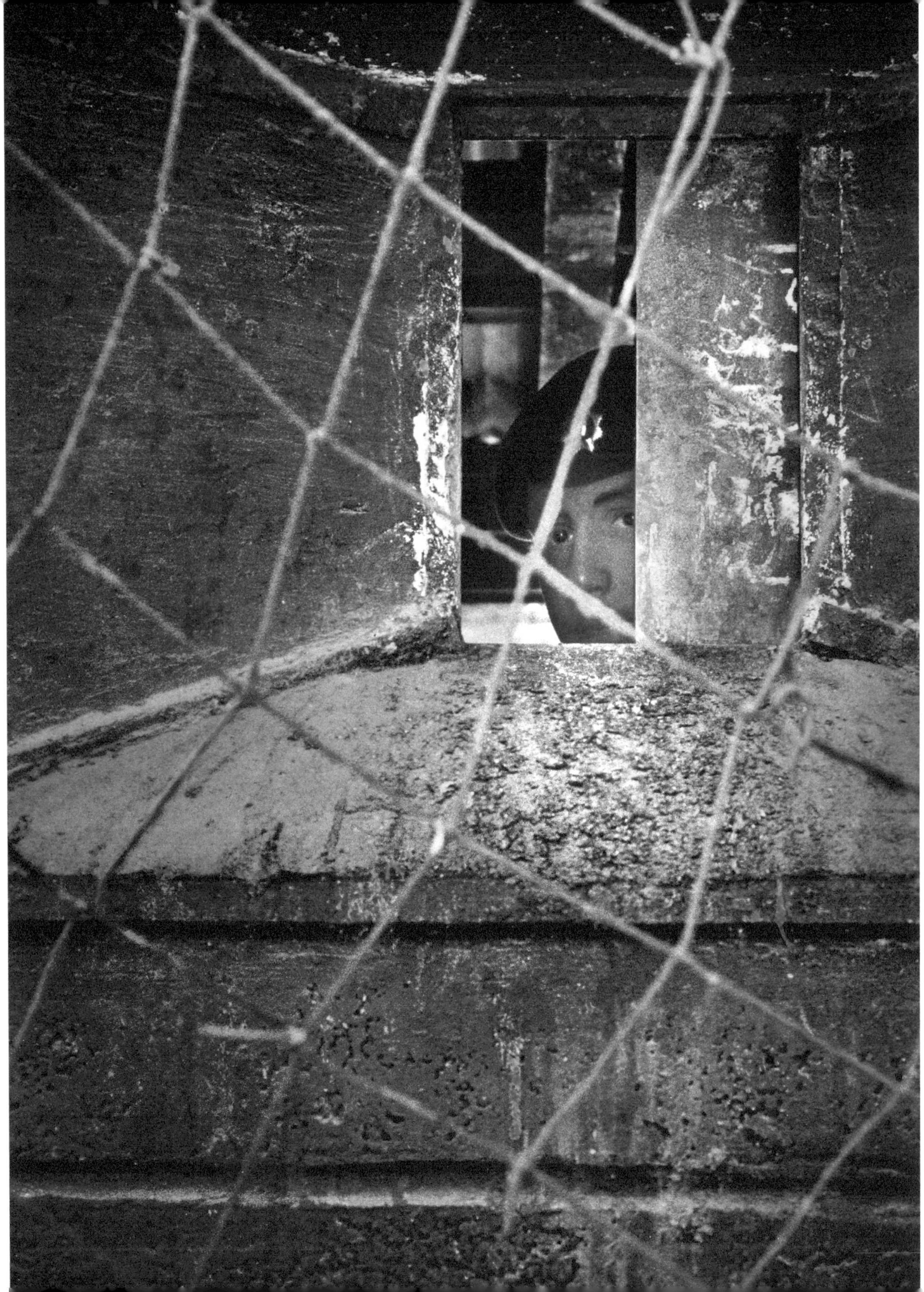

British soldier inside police station, West Belfast, Northern Ireland, 1982

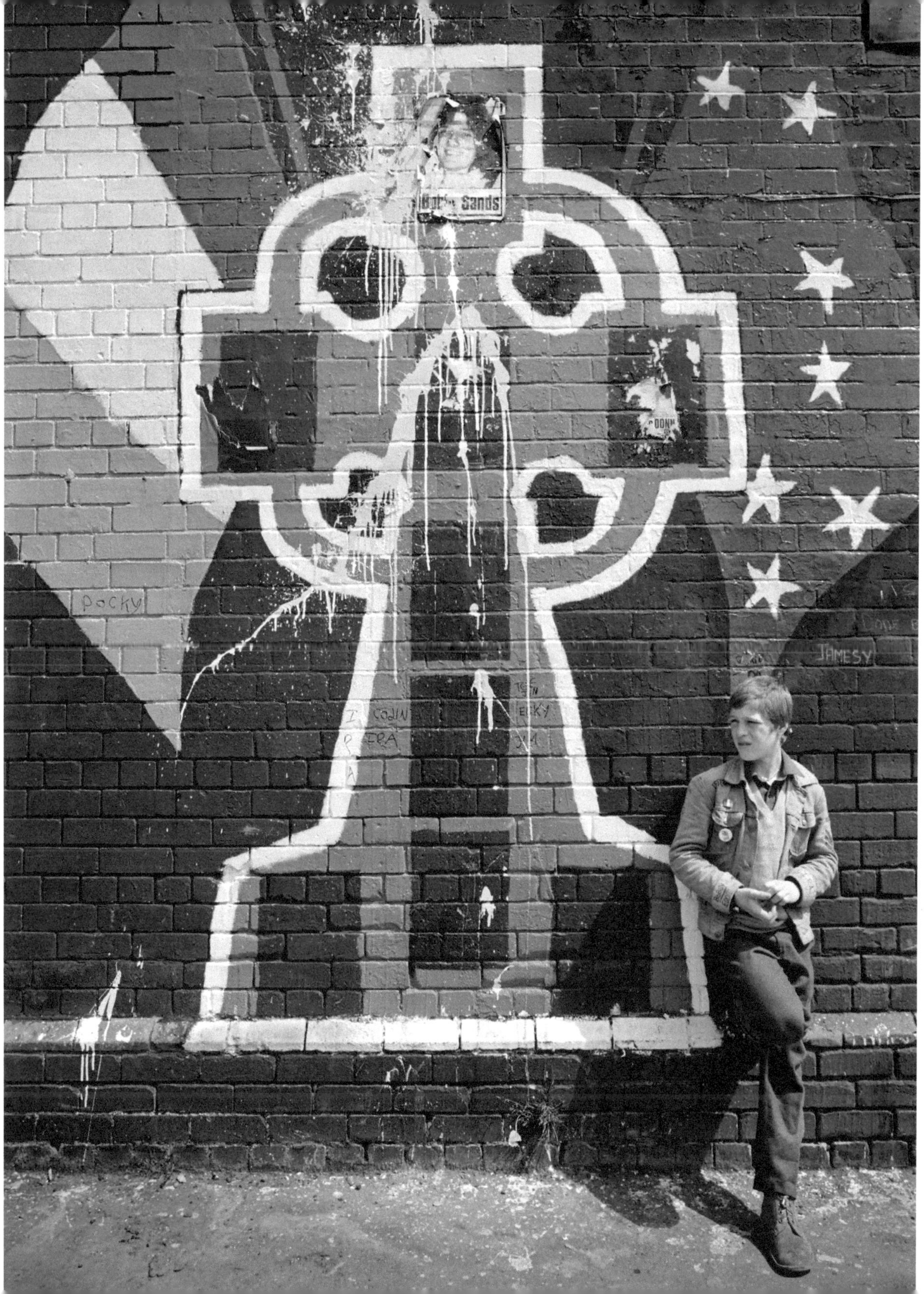

IRA wall mural,
West Belfast,
Northern Ireland, 1982

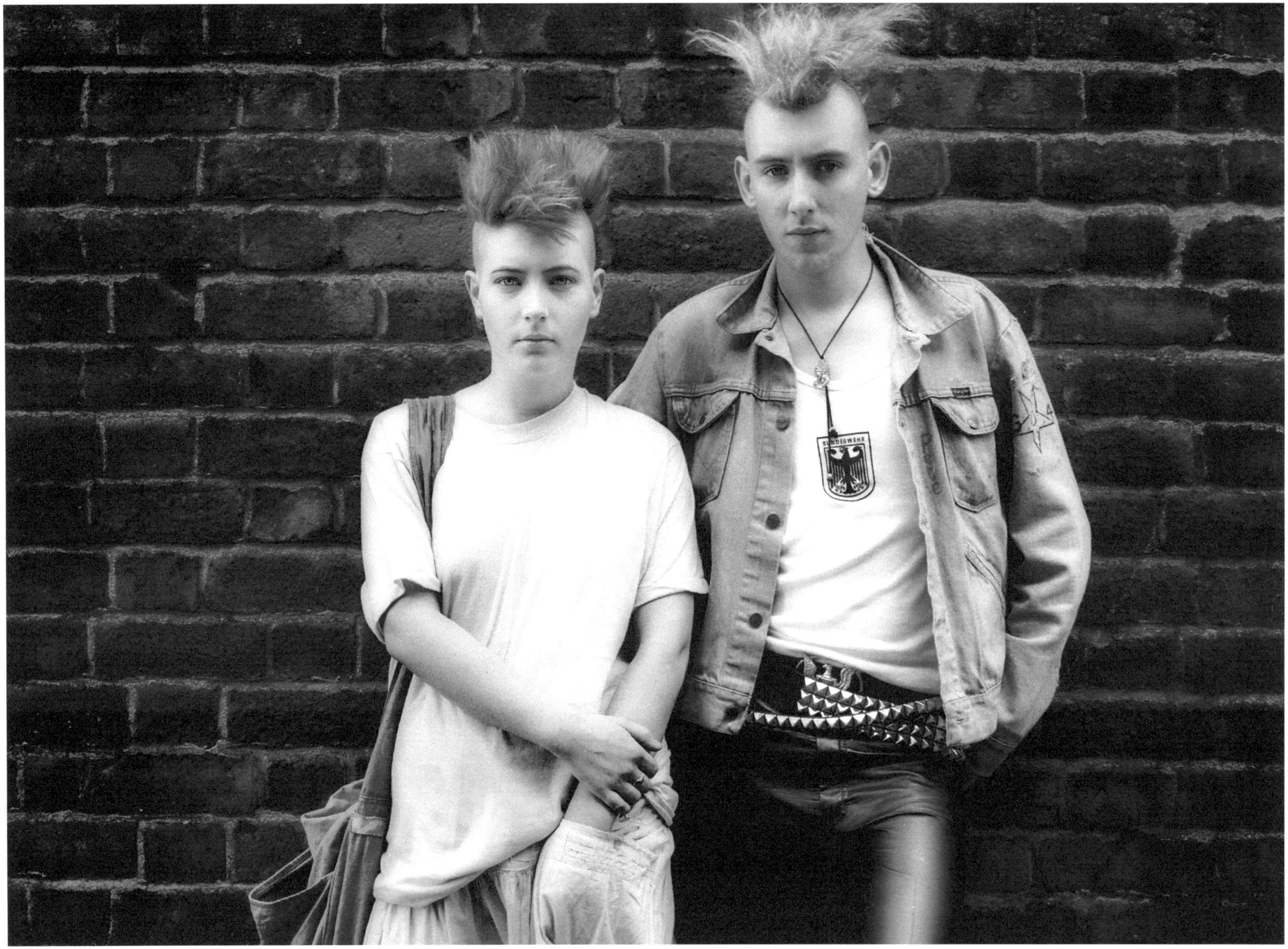

Great Victoria Street, Belfast,
Northern Ireland, 1984

People define history, and history defines people. UDA, Ulster Freedom Fighters, IRA, Provos, and SDLP—each group defined and confined the people of Northern Ireland. And then there were the outliers. The Punks were the disrupters of their day. They refused to be defined by either side. Harassed by Republicans and Loyalists alike, they sought to rip apart the social and political structures they were born into and create something completely different—a new subculture somewhere beyond the pale.

Acknowledgments

Paul Marion and Loom Press
Rosemary Noon and the Noon family
Stephen O'Connor
Peter H. Burke
Donna and Bernie Spellissy
Malachy Daly, our Northern Ireland connection
George Laffan, Irish sculptor—gone but not forgotten
Joan Ross, graphic designer
Pookiesnackenburger, street band
The Russell Brothers, storytellers and renown musicians

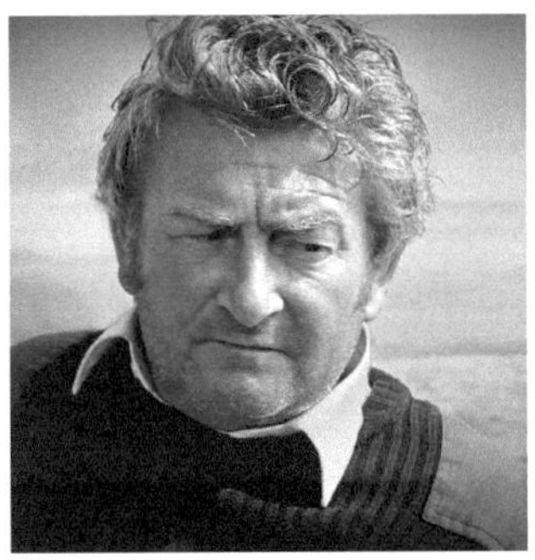

RIP Joe Roddy, one of the original watermen of Ireland

"A surprised murmur quickly turns to gasps of shock and awe as more heads turn and look out to sea at the dark mysterious Christ-like apparition standing on water fast approaching them. Joe was greeted by stunned silence from the astonished crowd. He fondly recalls seeing nothing but 'the whites of their eyes and their gobs smacked wide open,' as he stepped onto the beach and into the history books to arguably become Ireland's first surfer."

—Wayne Murphy, *Carve Surfing Magazine*, 2/28/19